Manifesto For Breaking The Financial Slavery To Interest

by

Gottfried Feder

Translated with a Preface

by

Alexander Jacob

Manifesto For Breaking The
Financial Slavery To Interest
by
Gottfried Feder

Translated with a Preface
by
Alexander Jacob

ISBN-13: 978-1-910881-07-1

Black House Publishing Ltd
Kemp House
152 City Road
London
UNITED KINGDOM
EC1V 2NX

www.blackhousepublishing.com
Email: info@blackhousepublishing.com

Contents

Preface - Alexander Jacob   3

Manifesto For The Breaking Of The Financial Slavery To Interest   11

Explanation And Justification   15

The Conversion Of War Bonds Into Bank Assets   40

Special Explanations Of The Legal Demand In The Manifesto   42

The Objections And Their Refutation   47

Further Programme   61

Select Bibliography   63

Preface

by Alexander Jacob

Gottfried Feder was born in 1883 in Würzburg and studied engineering at the Technical Universities in Munich, Berlin and Zurich. After the completion of his studies he set up a construction company of his own in 1908 under the aegis of Ackermann and Co. and undertook several projects in Bulgaria. From 1917 onwards he taught himself financial politics and economics and, in late 1918, not long after the proclamation of the Weimar Republic by Philipp Scheidemann in November of that year,[1] Feder wrote the present manifesto on usury and sent it to the Kurt Eisner government although he obtained no response. The Treaty of Versailles signed in June 1919 which determined Germany as solely responsible for the war and liable to reparations caused Feder to fear that Germany was now firmly in the hands of the international financiers. In September of that year, Feder established a militant league (Kampfbund) for the breaking of interest slavery and the nationalisation of the state bank. His anti-capitalism was bound also to racialism insofar as the international financiers were considered to be mostly Jews. His nationalist efforts thus drew him into a close alliance with Anton Drexler and Dietrich Eckart and the three together formed the Deutsche Arbeiter Partei, which was the forerunner of the NSDAP. Adolf Hitler and Ernst Röhm soon joined the party and the name of the party was changed by Hitler to Nationalsozialistische Deutsche Arbeiterpartei (NSDAP).

Hitler also attended Feder's lectures on economic subjects and wrote later in his *Mein Kampf* (1925/6) that he perceived in Feder's arguments "a theoretical truth that must have enormous significance for the future of the German people ... For the first time in my life I began a major examination of the international stock-exchange and loan capital". Indeed, in the Foreword to Feder's Der deutsche Staat (1923), Hitler wrote that in Feder's work the National Socialist movement had acquired its "catechism".

In 1920, Hitler, along with Feder and Drexler, composed the '25 point Programme' of the NSDAP. This programme rejected the Treaty of Versailles and called for a reunification of German peoples along with

---

1   See below p51.

3

an exclusion of aliens, especially Jews, from national life. In February 1920, Hitler held a rally in which he presented the programme to the German people. Later, in 1927, Feder published a comprehensive version of the programme entitled *Das Programm der NSDAP and seine weltanschaulichen Grundlagen.*[2] In 1923, Feder produced a further elaboration of his national economic views entitled *Der deutsche Staat auf nationaler und sozialer Grundlage*, which is indeed his major work.

Feder took part in Hitler's failed Beer Hall Putsch against the Bavarian government in 1923 but was only fined 50 marks for unlawful assumption of authority since he had acted, for a day, as the new "finance minister". In 1924, he was elected a representative to the parliament. In parliament, he demanded the confiscation of Jewish property and the freezing of interest-rates. which were key elements of the anti-capitalist programme of the party. In 1931, Feder was appointed chairman of the economic council of the NSDAP but gradually, under pressure from big industrialists like Gustav Krupp, Fritz Thyssen and Emil Kirdorf, Hitler decided to distance himself from Feder's socialist ideas.[3] With Hitler's strategic alliance with big industrialists and capital, even foreign capital, for his intended war on Bolshevism, Feder lost most of his influence on the party since foreign banks especially would not have supported Feder's plans for a nationalised interest-free banking system. The loss of interest in Feder's economic policies among the party members is evidenced in Hans Reupke's book *Der Nationalsozialismus und die Wirtschaft* (!931) where the author stated that it was no longer necessary to deal with the "breaking of interest slavery" in "the extreme form in which it first emerged".[4]

Thus, when Hitler assumed power in 1933, Feder was not named Economics Minister but rather only State Secretary in the Economics Ministry. However, Feder published in 1933 a collection of his essays entitled *Kampf gegen die Hochfinanz* as well as a book on the Jews called *Die Juden*. In 1934, the influential banker Hjalmar Schact was made Economics Minister since his contacts with the big

---

2   This work was translated by E.T.S. Dugdale as *The Programme of the NSDAP and its general conceptions*, Munich, 1932.

3   For the part played by big industries in Hitler's rise to power see G. Hallgarten, "Adolf Hitler and German heavy industry 1931-1933", *Journal of Economic History*, 12 (1952).

4   H. Reupke, *Der Nationalsozialismus und die Wirtschaft*, Berlin, 1931, pp.29ff.

industrialists made him more useful to Hitler in his rearmament aims than Feder with his stark anti-capitalist doctrines. Feder's subordination to Hjalmar Schacht was indeed a concrete sign of his fall from grace. After the Knight of the Long Knives in 1934, when left-wing nationalists like Gregor Strasser were assassinated, Feder withdrew from the government. In 1936, he was given a new job as professor at the Technical University in Berlin which he maintained until his death in 1941.

Feder's analysis of the desperate economic condition of Germany and other states after the war led him to believe that this was due primarily to the loan of credit at interest by international financiers. In order to render a state autarkic, the state must create its own money free of interest and the concomitant taxes. This money would be covered through the public productive activities of the state such as transport, power plants, armaments, etc. This does not mean the nationalisation of personal or industrial property but rather the securing of the latter from the burden of interest normally attached to loan capital. Industrial capital is thus to be favoured at the expense of loan capital. Feder's theory thus provided a robust answer to Marxism, which had conveniently neglected the question of interest in its constant focus on class-warfare.

However, the economic theories of Feder were not all closely followed by the National Socialist state after 1933, when economic policy was determined first by the banker Hjalmar Schacht and, from 1936, by Hermann Göring, who was placed in full control of the rearmament of the Reich under the second Four Year Plan.[5] The Nationalist Socialist state at first sought to combat the cumulative deflation by the creation of money and work.[6] Work was created by increasing public works activity, such as notably the building of super- highways, and agricultural projects. This is of course in consonance with Feder's doctrines. The need to increase the money supply is also detectable in Feder's programme since one of the reasons of his injunction to do away with interest was to make more money available for state expenditures. However, the major purpose of the production of money already from 1934 seems to have been rearmament, and front

---

5   At Göring's request, Schacht resigned from his post as Minister of Economics in December 1937 while he remained President of the Reichsbank until January 1939, when he was dismissed from that position too by Hitler.

6   See G. Senft, "Anti-Kapitalismus von Rechts? - Eine Abrechnung mit Gottfried Feders 'Brechung der Zinsknechtschaft'", Zeitschrift für Sozialökonomie, 106 (1995), pp.18-32.

companies, such as Schacht's Metallurgische Forschungsgesellschaft (Mefo), were formed to accept monies from the well-known industrialists such as Krupp, Siemens, etc. and transfer them to the production of armaments. Burton Klein attempted to show that the degree of rearmament was at first not one geared to any "total war" but only to a limited war mainly oriented to the transformation of the eastern neighbours of Germany into a buffer region against the Bolshevik menace.[7] However, the replacement of Schacht by Göring suggests that, already in 1936, Hitler was indeed preparing for a major war. Thus it happened that, although the state sought to avoid inflation through the imposition of strict price-, wage- and tax-regulations and although the public enterprises of the state succeeded in reducing unemployment,[8] the money in circulation in the Reich gradually grew in direct proportion to its military enterprises, from 3.5 billion in 1933 to 73 billion in 1945, when the war had indeed become "total". In the end the economy naturally could not resist the onset of a disastrous inflation.[9]

Feder's autarkic theories were not particularly novel in Germany since Adam Müller (1779-1829) had propounded an anti-liberal anti-free-trade nationalist economics already in the early 19th century and his influence may be detected even in the corporatist theories of the Austrian Othmar Spann (1878-1950) in the early 20th century. Other protectionist economic theoreticians in Austria included Joseph Schlesinger (1830-1901) and Wenzel Schober (1846-1928), and Feder expressly cited the latter's doctrines as a forerunner of his own.[10] Rudolf Hilferding (1877-1941), the Marxist economist of the Sozialdemokratische Partei Deutschlands (SPD) too had pointed before Feder to the difference between productive industrial capital and parasitical loan capital.

Another economist who vaguely resembled Feder was Silvio Gsell

---

7   See B.H. Klein, *Germany's Economic Preparations For War*, Harvard University Press, 1968; cf. A.S. Milward, *The German Economy At War*, London, 1965 .

8   For a brief and relatively balanced account of the economic recovery under Hitler's Reich see R.J. Overy, *The Nazi Economic Recovery 1932-1938*, Cambridge: CUP, 1996, especially Ch.4, where the author ascribes the revival to "the control of trade, the intervention in the capital market, high levels of investment and a rapid return to full employment" (p.36) effected under "a complete system" (p.38) of interdependent state controls.

9   See G. Senft, *op.cit.*

10   G. Feder, *Der deutsche Staat*, 1935, p.63.

(1862-1930), the cosmopolitan socialist who propounded a "natural" economy that would reward work by removing all inherited privileges and interest and rent charges. Gsell was appointed Finance Representative of the Bavarian Soviet Republic though his tenure lasted only 7 days. Feder soon recognised that Gsell had made common cause with the "Jewish bloodhounds"[11] whereas his own economic doctrines were marked by a steady focus on the Jewish sources of financial capitalism. Besides, Gsell was not averse to credit, which he saw as necessary for economic development, whereas Feder considered credit as "the trick, the trap into which our entire economy entered" (see below p.47). Feder's programme was opposed to the Communist form of socialism insofar as he wished to guarantee private property while expressly prohibiting real estate speculation such as was carrried out by the Jews. Besides, unlike Gsell's socialised land that could be leased by any person, including Jewish immigrants, Feder's conception of land ownership was strictly restricted to Germans.

Feder designed his manifesto as an answer to the Communist Manifesto which Karl Marx and Friedrich Engels had published in 1848 for, just as the latter ended with the words "Proletarians of all lands, unite!", so too does Feder end his with the words "Workers of all lands, unite!". However, in opposition to the Marxist focus on class-struggle, Feder's chief target in his manifesto is the evil of interest and the capacity of interest to allow men to enjoy a steadily growing supply of money without work. Feder points continuously to the difference between "schaffendes" and "raffendes" capital, that is productive and money-hoarding capital. Thus, like the National Socialists, he was not entirely anti-capitalist but rather opposed to the Jewish high finance which conducted its international games with loan capital and interest to the ruinous detriment of individual states.[12]

His principal steps against the evil of usury are the nationalisation of the state and other large banks and the abolition of interest on all public debts. The state bank must reserve the right to print money. The financing of all essential public works will be carried out through the issuance of interest-free bank certificates. These certificates will be repaid from the profits of the new enterprises. It is true that Feder was not trained as an expert in economics except through self-instruction and the Marxist professor Erik Nölting criticised him in

---

11   G. Feder, *Der deutsche Staat*,1923, p.71.

12   For the dependence of the Weimar Republic on foreign capital, especially from the United States, see R.J. Overy, *op.cit.*, pp.11ff.

1931 for propounding a theory that would lead to hyperinflation.[13] However, the inflation that may be generated by a state bank is more controllable than that induced by the creation of money by private credit banks since the issuance of new money may be more strictly controlled by the state.[14] The removal of interest from the state bank certificates would further render the return of monies to the bank easier. Also, the use of the newly created money for public purposes such as highways and schools creates ideal values that bear long term benefits for the state. The ruling principle of the Feder's economy is indeed the socialist one of "Gemeinnutz vor Eigennutz" or "the public interest before personal interest". Only on such a basis can the nation maintain its financial and social independence.

The international dimensions of the problem of the existing high finance are pointed to already at the beginning of Feder's manifesto when he identifies the prime evil to be attacked as "Mammonism", which he defines as

> One, the overpowering international financial powers, the supra-national financial power enthroned above the self-determination of all nations, the international high finance, the unique Golden International;

> Two, a frame of mind that has taken control of the widest sphere of nations, the insatiable greed for acquisition, the life-view which is purely oriented to the this-worldly that has already led, and must lead further, to a frightful lowering of all moral conceptions. (p.11)

The modus operandi of Mammonism is the financing of the imperialistic ambitions of the Anglo-American alliance:

> The big financial powers indeed hide as the ultimate driving force behind the world-encompassing Anglo-American imperialism; nothing else. The big financial powers have indeed financed the frightful massacre of the world war. The big financial powers have, as the owners of all the big newspapers, indeed entangled the world in a net of lies ... the spirit of Mammonism, which wanted

---

13   "Sozialdemokratie und Nationalsozialismus: Gespräch auf die deutschen Welle am 3. Jan. 1931 zwischen Prof. Erik Nölting von der Akademie der Arbeit, Frankfurt a. M., Mitglied d. Pr. Landtags, und dem nat. soz. Reichstagsabg. Dip. Ing. Gottfr. Feder", in *Kampf gegen die Hochfinanz,* Munich, 1933.

14   See the web log by "Scanners", "Gottfried Feder und das zinlose Geld", www.utopia.de/blog/umweltpolitik/gottfried-feder-und-das-zinslose.

to know only more export figures, national wealth (expansion, big bank projects, international financing) led to a collapse of public morality, to the sinking of our ruling circles into materialism and hedonism, to a flattening of our cultural life, all factors that are complicit in the frightful collapse. (p.17)

The source of the financial power of the Mammonistic bosses is the interest paid to loan capital.

The Bolshevists too had proposed an answer to capitalism but Feder terms this a "quack treatment" which does not deal with the "internal poisoning" of the financial system but merely attacks anybody who profits from it. Thus it has created an invidious cleavage between employers and workers and proffered a blind solution wherein everything is shared by everybody and the natural satisfaction of personal possession is denied to the people. As he puts it:

this [the Communist idea that everything should belong to everybody] ... then finally ends and results in the fact that everybody has – nothing. Hunger, desperation, misery, illness and distress have set in in Russia, men have lost the last part of their courage to live and joy in living. (p.57)

The worst fault of the Communist system is that it has ignored the difference between loan capital and industrial capital and that, he suggests, may have been deliberate, since the Marxist movement has been dominated by members of a certain race.[15] He quotes from Disraeli himself to stress the importance of the racial question in the understanding of economic history. And, in his conclusion to the work, he plainly identifies Mammonism with Judaism itself, a religion in which the Jewish god promises to his people: "I will give you all the treasures of the world as your own, all the nations should lie at your feet, and you shall rule over them".

Although Feder did not succeed in maintaining an influential role in the National Socialist government, Feder's early manifesto remains a noteworthy document in the history of modern economics both for its sharp focus on interest as the root of the evil of international finance capitalism and for its subtle identification of the Jewish domination of economics, whether Capitalist or Communist, as the ultimate cause of the debilitation of individual nations.

---

15   See below p.15..

The Manifesto

Mammonism is the heavy, all-encompasing and all-constricting sickness from which our cultured world, nay all mankind, suffers. It is like a devastating epidemic, a consuming poison that has taken hold of the nations of the world.

By Mammonism is to be understood:

> One, the overpowering international financial powers, the supranational financial power enthroned above the self-determination of all nations, the international high finance, the unique Golden International;

> Two, a frame of mind that has taken control of the widest sphere of nations, the insatiable greed for acquisition, the life-view which is purely oriented to the this-worldly that has already led, and must lead further, to a frightful lowering of all moral conceptions.

This frame of mind is embodied and carried to an extreme in international plutocracy.

The chief power source of Mammonism is the effortless and endless flow of goods that is produced by interest.

From the thoroughly unethical idea of loan interest rate was born the Golden International. The intellectual and moral frame of mind developed from the greed for interest and usury of every sort has led one part of the bourgeoisie into a quagmire.

The idea of interest is the diabolical invention of loan capital, it alone makes possible the sluggish drone-life of a minority of financial powers at the cost of the productive nations and their workforce, it has led to the deep unbridgeable oppositions, to the class-hatred from which are born civil and fratricidal war.

A sole remedy, the radical remedy for the healing of suffering mankind is the breaking of the financial slavery to interest

The breaking of the financial slavery to interest signifies the sole possible and final liberation of productive work from the secret overpowering financial powers.

11

The breaking of the financial slavery to interest means the re-establishment of the free personality, the liberation of man from enslavement, from the magic spell in which his soul was bound by Mammonism. One who wishes to combat capitalism must break the interest slavery.

Where should the breaking of interest slavery begin? With loan capital!

Why?

Because loan capital is so overpowering in comparison with all industrial large capital that the big financial powers can be combated only through the breaking of the interest slavery of loan capital. 20:1 is the ratio of loan capital to industrial large capital. The German nation must raise every year over 12 billion in interest for the loan capital in the form of direct and indirect taxes, house rents and life-insurance, whereas indeed in the economic boom years of the war the entire sum of all the dividends gathered from the German public companies amounted to only 1 billion.

Overstepping all possible human calculation – the avalanche-like growth of loan capital through an eternal, endless and effortless flow of goods from interest and compound interest.

Now, what blessing does the breaking of interest slavery bring to the working people of Germany, for the proletarians of all the countries of the world?

The breaking of interest slavery brings gives us the possibility of effecting the abolition of all direct and indirect taxes. Listen, you value-producing men of all countries, states and continents, all the state revenues flowing from direct and indirect sources flow fully into the pockets of big loan capital.

The proceeds of the state business institutions such as the post, telegraph, telephone, railways, mining works, forests, etc., are entirely sufficient to be able to defray therefrom all the necessary state responsibilities for education, development, administration of justice, administration and social welfare.

Thus all true socialism will bring no blessing to humanity so long as the proceeds from the non-profit institutions remain tributary to large loan capital.

So we first demand as a basic state law for the German peoples, and then as the basic law for all those fraternal peoples who wish to enter with us into the cultural community of a federation of nations, the following:

1. The war-bonds as well as all the other debt instruments of the German Reich, and all the other debt instruments of the German federal states, especially railway bonds, further the debt requirements of all self-governing bodies are declared, with the abolition of interest, to be legal currency, notional amounts.

2. In the case of all the other fixed interest securities, bonds, industrial obligations, mortgages, etc., there enters, in place of interest, repayment; therewith, after 20 or 25 years, the loan capital is, in accordance with the level of interest, paid off and the debt is resolved.

3. All real estate debts, mortgages, are, according to the burdens entered in the land register, paid off as before in instalments. The wealth in houses and landed property freed in this way becomes partially the property of the state or of the self-governing body. In this way the state finds itself in a position to determine and reduce the rent prices.

4. The entire monetary system stands under the central state treasury. All private banks such as postal cheque services, savings banks and credit unions are registered as branches.

5. All collateral loans are forgiven only by the state bank. All personal and merchandise credit is ceded to private bankers with a state licence. The latter is granted to certain districts under consideration of the question of need, and with a prohibition of the establishment of branches. The fee-scale is determined by the state.

6. The dividend values are redeemed at annual rates of 5% in the same way as the fixed-interest securities. The excess profit proceeds are partially paid out as compensation for "risk capital" (in contrast to the fixed-interest or gilt-edged securities) to the share-holders, while the further surplus is, through the independent right of the workers, either socially distributed or used for the reduction of the prices of products.

7. To all persons who, for physical reasons (old age, sickness, bodily or mental inability to work, extreme youth), are not in a position to earn their livelihood the interest proceeds from existing wealth, which up to now could even possibly be raised, will, on delivery of the securities, continue to be paid as life-annuities.

8. In the interest of the reduction of the existing inflation through means of payment a general, strongly phased, confiscation will be undertaken of assets that are held in war bonds or other debts of the Reich or the states. These securities will be destroyed.

9. Through extremely intensive popular education it is to be made clear to the people that money is not and should not be anything but an acknowledgement of performed work, since every highly developed financial economy indeed requires money as a means of exchange, but that therewith is also completed the function of money and that in no case can an otherworldly power be granted to money through interest to grow beyond itself into a burden of productive work.

Why have we not up to now achieved all this which is so self-evident, which one must call a Columbus egg[16] as regards the social question?

Because in our blinding by Mammonism we have forgotten how to see clearly, that the doctrine of the sacredness of interest is an enormous self-deception, that the gospel of interest as the only blessing has entangled our entire thought in the golden nets of the international plutocracy. Because we have forgotten - and are deliberately held in uncertainty about it by the all-powerful financial powers - that, with the exception of a few financially powerful people, the supposedly wonderful interest that is so loved by the unthinking is completely consumed by taxes.

Our entire state tax legislation is and remains, so long as we do not have a liberation from interest slavery, only an obligation to high finance, and not what we often imagine - voluntary sacrifice for the realisation of communal work.

16   [A Columbus egg is a good idea that is obvious but not perceived by the majority.] [N.B. All notes in brackets are by the translator.]

For this reason is the liberation from interest slavery the clear solution for the world revolution, for the liberation of productive work from the shackles of the supra-national financial powers.

Explanation and justification

We stand in the midst of one of the most severe crises which our poor nation has to weather out in an extremely distressing history. Our nation is seriously ill, the whole world is seriously ill. The people stutter helplessly; an ardent longing, a cry for redemption goes through the dark masses. The people try to find themselves through laughter and dance, through the cinema and parades. As if senselessly deceiving themselves about their own wretched fate. Deceiving themselves about their betrayed hopes, deceiving themselves about the deep inner sorrow resulting from the frightful disappointment about that which people are wont to term "the accomplishments of the revolution". But how differently did one imagine everything, how different did all the fine promises sound, everything seemed to be glistening gold that one hoped to pick up in the night there, in the darkness of our military collapse, and now, when the gray day illumines the trove, they are just decayed pieces of wood. Now we stand there helplessly, for the sake of these decayed pieces of wood which shone so beautifully in the night we have thrown away everything that up to now was near and dear to us, and we have crammed all our bags with this wretched find. No wonder that the rage of desperation has seized precisely the poorest of the poor and that they rage in senseless fury against their own brothers and try to destroy everything that stands in their way in their deep longing for liberation. This condition must lead to a total madness if unscrupulousness and stupidity whips up the populace further, and where this madness leads we see in Bolshevist Russia. Nationalisation, as socialisation is termed in Russia, has shown itself to be a failure, Lenin announces placidly. The economy is destroyed, the purchasing power of money almost null, the intelligentsia slain, the worker without bread. Desperation in the entire nation; only bloody Terror supported by Mongol and Latvian mercenary troops can protect the Red dictators from the revenge of the disappointed people. Even among us the development will take this route if we continue to keep in our government international speculators, drilled party fanatics, representatives of the bourgeoisie which has been most severely burdened and members of a race that is fundamentally different from the German people. But what were all the fine, fine words that were whispered into our ears: the peace of rapprochement, League of

Nations, parliamentarianism, sovereignty of the people, democracy, dictatorship of the proletariat, socialism, destruction of capitalism, liberation from militarism, and whatever all the fine catchwords may be. A new free people was to have arisen that would determine its destiny by itself. Nothing of all that has become true, could not become true, can never become true, if we do not go into all these phenomena, all these catchwords with the highest moral seriousness, if we do not, like a clever benevolent doctor, conscientiously examine the symptoms of the illness and discover with the greatest care the present condition of the sick person, and spare no pains to determine from whence this serious critical illness comes.

Mammonism Is The Illness Of Our Age.

What is Mammonism?

Mammonism is the sinister invisible secret rule of the big international financial powers. But Mammonism is also a frame of mind, it is the worship of these financial powers on the part of all those have been infected with the Mammonistic poison. Mammonism is the immoderate extension of man's instinct of acquisition, which is in itself healthy. Mammonism is the greed for money that has become a mania, that knows no higher goal than piling up money on money, that seeks with a brutality without equal to force all the powers of the world into its service and that must lead to the economic enslavement, to the exploitation of the workers of all the nations of the world. Mammonism is the intellectual condition that has led to a lowering of all moral conceptions. Considered as a world phenomenon it is to be identified with brutal ruthless egoism in man. Mammonism is the spirit of avarice, of boundless domination, the mentality oriented only to the acquisition of the property and wealth of the world; it is fundamentally the religion of the type of man solely oriented to this world. Mammonism is the exact opposite of socialism. Socialism, conceived of as an extremely high moral idea, as the idea that man is not in this world only for himself alone, that every man has duties towards society, towards all mankind, and not only that, that he is not only responsible for the momentary welfare of his family, his racial comrades, his nation but that he also has unavoidable moral obligations towards the future of his children and his nation.

More concretely we must consider Mammonism as the conscious co-operation of the power-hungry capitalists of all nations. In this the veiled appearance of Mammonism is always noteworthy.

The big financial powers indeed hide as the ultimate driving force behind the world-encompassing Anglo-American imperialism; nothing else. The big financial powers have indeed financed the frightful massacre of the world war. The big financial powers have, as the owners of all the big newspapers, indeed entangled the world in a net of lies. They have whipped up with pleasure all the lower passions, have carefully cultivated existing trends, have raised the French idea of revanchism to a boiling point with skilful press propaganda, carefully nourished the pan-Slavist idea, the arrogance of Serbia as a great power and the financial need of these states in which the world conflagration had to be ignited. Even among us in Germany the spirit of Mammonism, which wanted to know only more export figures, national wealth (expansion, big bank projects, international financing) led to a collapse of public morality, to the sinking of our ruling circles into materialism and hedonism, to a flattening of our cultural life, all factors that are complicit in the frightful collapse.

We must ask ourselves in amazement from where Mammonism, international high finance gets its irresistible power.

It is not at all to be overlooked that the international co-operation of the big financial powers represents a rather new phenomenon. We have no equivalent for it in all of history. International liabilities of a monetary sort were as good as unknown. Only with the emerging world economy, with the general world traffic did the idea of the international interest business establish itself and here we touch the deepest root, here we have hit upon the innermost power-source from which the Golden International sucks its irresistible power.

It is interest, the effortless and endless flow of wealth through mere possession of money without putting in any work that has allowed the great powers to grow. Interest is the diabolical principle out of which the Golden International was born. Loan capital has attached itself to everything everywhere. As if with octopus arms, big loan capital has ensnared all the states, all the nations of the world.

State debentures, state bonds, railway bonds, war bonds, mortgages, bond certificate obligations, in short loan instruments of all sorts, have ensnared our entire economic life in such a way that henceforth

17

the peoples of the world struggle helplessly in the golden net. For the sake of the interest principle, following a conception of the state that is basically false, that every sort of possession has a right to profit, we have given ourselves up to the financial slavery to interest. Not a single real cogent moral reason can be cited for the claim that mere possession of money provides a right to lasting interest profits.

This inner opposition to interest and income of any sort without the emergence of productive work pervades the spiritual life of all peoples. But never has this deep inner resistance to the power of money become so conscious to the peoples as in our age. Never has Mammonism prepared itself in such a world-encompassing way to assume world rule. Never yet has it placed in its service all baseness (the striving for the base in men), greed for power, greed for revenge, rapacity, envy and lies in such a cunningly disguised and still brutally aggressive way as now. In its deepest aspect the world war is one of the great decisive points in the development process of mankind, in the battle to decide whether in the future the mammonistic-materialistic world-view or the socialistic-aristocratic will determine the fate of the world.

Externally, the mammonistic Anglo-American coalition has for now doubtlessly won. As a reaction against it Bolshevism has risen in the East and, if one wishes to consider Bolshevism a major idea, it is doubtless a standpoint diametrically opposed to the mammonistic world-view. The methods that Bolshevism seeks to adopt for this are however attempted quack treatments. They are an attempt to help a patient suffering from an internal poisoning with a scalpel, through amputation of the head, arm and legs.

To this raging of Bolshevism, this senseless upheaval we must oppose a planned new idea that unites all working classes with a unifying force in order to drive out the poison that has made the world sick.

This method I see in the breaking of the financial slavery to interest. There are three factors that allow interest of loan capital to appear as the real, the true cause of our financial misery.

First, the enormous imbalance of fixed-interest loan capital, therefore of capital which without adequate productive work grows from itself and indeed continues to grow forever. This loan capital has among us in Germany already reached a height that we do not value too high at 250 billion. Against this monstrous sum there stands only a sum of 11.8 billion as the industrial working capital of our entire German industry. In addition to it there is the capital of 3.5 billion of the 16000 limited companies so that we have altogether only some 15 billion of industrial total capital to record. 20:1 is the first fundamental finding. This finding implies that all measures that deal with financial problems of the greatest sort must from the point of view of loan capital show themselves to be 20 times more effective than measures that are directed against industrial large capital.

Second, the interest of the loan capitals estimated above at 250 billion amounts, taken as a whole, to some 12.5 billion a year for all time. The total sum of all dividends gathered in 1916 amounted in 1915 to around 1 billion marks. In the preceding decades this figure was on average around 600 million. It may perhaps have risen in the last two war years still more significantly higher, but on the other hand it will show in the current year so much greater a fall.

The average profitability of all German public companies was 8.21%, thus only around 3.5% higher than the average profit of the fixed-interest bond values.

So I repeat, in future the German people will have to pay around 12.5 billion for the diverse eternal interests of large loan capital whereas the profit from industrial capital in the biggest boom year was 1 billion, in times of undisturbed economic activity only 0.6 billion, thus we see here too once again a dimension ratio of 20:1 up to 12:1.

The third and most dangerous factor is the monstrous growth of large loan capital surpassing all comprehension through interest and compound interest. I must here elaborate further on something and hope to clarify the problem with a brief excursion into higher mathematics. First an example.

The charming history of the invention of chess is well known. The rich Indian king Sherham granted to the inventor as thanks for the invention of the royal game the fulfilment of a request. The request of the wise man was that the king would give him a grain of wheat on the first square of the chessboard, on the second two, on the third four and so on, on the following square the double of that on the previous square. The kind smiled at the apparently modest request of the wise man and ordered a bag of wheat to be brought to apportion the grains of wheat to each square. It is well known that the fulfilment of this request was impossible even for the richest prince of the world. All the harvests of the world would not suffice to fill the 64 squares of the chess board.

A further example: Many will still remember from their school-days the terrors of the calculation of compound interest; how the penny that is invested at compound interest at the time of the birth of Christ multiplies so that it doubles every 15 years. In the 15th year after Christ's birth the penny has grown to 2 pennies, in the 30th year after the birth of Christ to 4 pennies, in the 45th year after the birth of Christ to 8 pennies, and so on. They will at least remember what value this penny would represent today. Our entire earth made solidly of pure gold, our sun which is 1,297,000 times greater than our globe, all our planets glowing brightly of gold would not suffice to crush the value of this penny invested at compound interest.

A third example: The wealth of the Rothschild house, the oldest international plutocracy, is estimated today at around 40 billion. It is known that the old Amschel Mayer Rothschild[17] laid the foundation stone for the enormous wealth of his house in Frankfurt in 1800 without any wealth worth mentioning of his own through the loan of the millions that the Landgrave Wilhelm I of Hesse had given him for safekeeping.

If the growth of money through interest and compound interest had taken place only at the modest speed of the penny the curve would not have run so steeply. But supposing that the increase of wealth of the Rothschild's total wealth continues only at the speed of the penny the Rothschild wealth would in 1935 be 80 billion, in 1950 160 billion, in 1965 320 billion, and therewith surpass by far the entire German national wealth.

From these examples a mathematical law may be drawn. The curve that expresses the rise of the Rothschild wealth, the curve that may be drawn from the number of the grains of wheat on the chessboard, as well as the one that indicates the multiplication of the penny at compound interest, are simple mathematical curves. All these curves have the same character. After an initial modest and slow rise, the curve becomes ever sharper and soon practically approaches infinity at a tangent.

Quite differently on the other hand does the curve of industry capitals run. Also begun mostly with small beginnings there

---

17   [Amschel Mayer Rothschild (1744-1812), the founder of the Rothschild banking dynasty, was born in the Jewish ghetto of Frankfurt and gained his fortune as banker to the Landgrave, later Elector, Wilhelm of Hesse.]

appears soon a powerful rise of the curve until a certain saturation of capital is reached. Then the curves run flatter and will once again in general sink somewhat in the case of individual industries when new inventions have led to the devaluation of the existing factory installations, machines, etc. I would like to pick out only one example here, the development of the Krupp works. The old Krupp died in 1826 almost without any wealth. In 1855 Alfred Krupp received his first order for 36 cannons from the Egyptian government. In 1873 Krupp already employed 12,000 workers. In 1903 Mrs. Berta Krupp sold the entire works and grants for around 160 million to the Alfred Krupp public company. Today the share capital amounts to 250 million. What does the name Krupp signify for us Germans? The highpoint of our industrial development. The first cannon-builder in the world. An enormous amount of the most tenacious, goal-oriented and intensive work performance. For hundreds of thousands of our national comrades the Krupp undertaking meant bread and work. For our nation defence and weapons, and yet it is a dwarf compared to the Rothschild billions. What does the Krupp growth in one century signify compared to the growth of the Rothschild wealth from interest and compound interest through effortless and endless increase of value?

The two curves drawn in bold are loan interest curves and the upper curve shows the Rothschild wealth and the lower curve at first flat and then rapidly rising shows in general the characteristic development of all such curves in which the ordinates double on constant axes. The dotted line shows the development curve of our total industry in the course of the last 40-50 years. The finely differentiated dotted lines show the development of a series of randomly chosen large industrial undertakings, from which the general character of the dotted curve of industrial capital is derived.

It must be expressly noted that the curves are not shown to scale, that especially the curves of loan capital seem to a certain degree compressed together. So, for example, the curve of the Rothschild wealth in comparison to the Krupp curve would have to be set at least 80 times higher. The aim of the graph is indeed only to show the basically different character of the two curves. The curves of loan capital show at first a quite slowly rising development, then the development goes faster until, ever more furiously and pulling everything to itself, it then rises far above human conception and strives for infinity.

The curve of industrial capital on the other hand remains within the finite! The course may in individual cases show very strong deviations, but in general the character of industrial development will always be such that after a powerful initial development a certain period of maturity, of saturation follows, after which then slowly or quickly the downfall follows.

Nothing shows us more clearly the deep essential difference between loan capital and industrial capital. Nothing can make clearer to us the difference between the devastating effects of loan interest and the operating profits (dividends) of the risk working-capitals invested in large industrial enterprises.

It cannot be emphasised enough that the knowledge of the mathematical laws that are followed by loan capital and industrial capital alone shows us the clear way to where the lever is to be placed for a radical change of our shattered financial sector. We clearly recognise that it is not the capitalist economic order, not capital in itself, that is the scourge of mankind. The insatiable need of interest of large loan capital is the curse of the entire working mankind!

There must be capital – there must be work! Work alone can accomplish little – capital alone could do nothing!

Capital without work must be sterile! Therefore the most important demand, the noblest task of the revolution, the most reasonable aim of a world-revolution is the breaking of the financial slavery to interest.

The Rothschild house is today estimated at 40 billion. The billionaires of American high finance, Messrs Kahn, Loeb, Schiff, Speyer, Morgan, Vanderbilt, Astor are together estimated at at least 60-70 billion; with a mere 5 percent interest this means an income of these 8 families of 5-6 billion, that is almost as much, according to the researches of Helfferich in 1912,[18] as 75% of all that tax-payers in Prussia had as yearly income (There were at that time around 21,000,000 tax-payers. 75% of these around 15,000,000. For every tax-payer there are on average around 1.56 dependants, thus 23 million dependants.)

Thus around 38,000,000 have to live on what the above mentioned

---

18   Karl Helfferich (1872-1924) was a German economist and prominent member of the Deutschnationale Volkspartei (DNVP), the major nationalist party in Germany before the NSDAP. He was the author of *Deutschlands Wohlstand 1888-1913*, 1913.

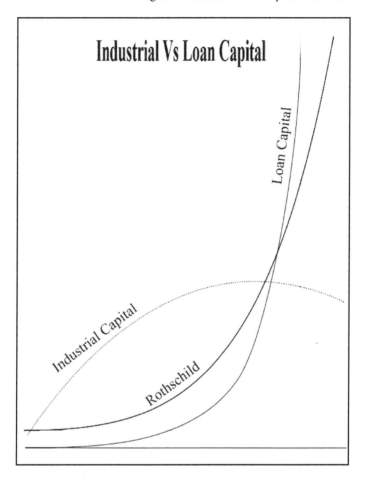

billionaires have as income in a year. - To be sure, the American billionaires are not pure loan capitalists in the sense that the Rothschild house, etc. are. I also do not want to argue on whether the American billionaires are "100 million dollar billionaires" or really "1000 million mark billionaires"; in the first case one must reckon one or two dozen more Croesuses. Or let us take simply the "300" of Rathenau[19], then our list will certainly be in order. And it is here not at all a question of giving a precise figure but the well-known scale of 300:38,000,000 opens our eyes to the powerful rule of the international loan capital.

---

19   Walther Rathenau (1867-1922) was a German Jewish industrialist and politician who served as Foreign Minister of the democratic Weimar Republic that was installed in 1919. He supported the Treaty of Versailles and was assassinated in June, 1922 by nationalist army officers.

Therefore let us shake off with one wrench these frightful shackles which must smother all work-based employment, let us tear away from money its power to bear interest and ever more interest until all of mankind has become totally subject in interest to international loan capital.

It is thus these three points that first made clear to us where alone the lever is to be placed for the alleviation of our internal financial distress. For another thing let us recognise that the assault of the entire socialist ideological world against industrial capital has fully failed, for a planned complete removal or socialisation of the entire entrepreneurial profit – on the condition that the economy is not weakened – would result in a laughably small amount measured against the enormous financial burdens of our Reich and state budget.

Through the breaking of the financial interest-slavery the entire financial misery can at one stroke be removed; all of a sudden we feel firm ground beneath our feet once again; all of a sudden must it and will it be clear to us that we have only lied to ourselves in a completely grotesque manner with this calamitous loan economy.

What then is a loan but debts! Loan capitals are debts! - that cannot be repeated too often. What sort of madness is it if the German people as a whole have pumped out 150 billion for its war, have promised to themselves an interest payment of 7.5 billion and find themselves placed in the quandary that was self-evident from the start of having to recover from themselves this 7.5 billion in the form of absolutely fantastic taxes. The tragic thing about this self-deception is however less the stupidity of the entire war loan economy with which we have with regard to other countries done ourselves proud as rather the fact that just a relatively small number of big capitalists derive an enormous profit from it and the entire working people, including the middle and small capitalists, and including trade, the professions and industry, must pay the interests. And here the political side of the entire idea comes to light, here they can recognise that in fact big loan capital and only this is the curse of the entire working mankind. One can twist and turn the matter as one wills, but always the mass of working people must in the final analysis bear the burden for the loan capital interests. The middle and small capitalists have nothing of their fine interests, can have nothing of them, for the interest amounts are to be totally removed from them. Either in the form of direct taxes or other constraints the working people are always the duped and large capital is the beneficiary.

It is now quite astonishing to see how the world of socialist ideas of Marx and Engels starting with the Communist Manifesto up to the Erfurt Programme (especially Kautsky)[20] and even the present-day socialist power-holders stop as if by command before the interests of loan capital. The sacredness of interest is a taboo; interest is the most sacred thing; nobody has yet dared to shake it; whereas property, nobility, personal and property security, the rights of the crown, reservations and religious conviction, officers' honour, fatherland and freedom are more or less free as a bird, interest is sacred and untouchable. The confiscation of wealth, socialisation are the order of the day, quite apparent legal breaches that are somewhat whitewashed only because they are supposedly perpetrated against the individual in the name of all; all that is permitted, but interest, interest is the "noli me tangere", the "touch me not". The subjection to interest of the Reich debt is the alpha and omega of the state budget. Its enormous weight drags the state ship into the abyss and yet – yes, it is all a swindle – an enormous self-deception fostered solely for the benefit of the great financial powers.

I should like here to touch briefly on the objections that will be dealt with later with regard to the small pensioner so that one does not remain hanging in thought about that. These do not come into consideration in the observation of the very big questions and it is quite self-evident that these compensations should be provided for by the greatest expansion of social insurance.

'Swindle', I said, interest swindle! a harsh word. But if this word, which was indeed the one most used during the war on the field and in the homeland, has a justification, it has a justification mostly for the interest swindle.

But how was it with the war bonds? The Reich took out of the pockets of the people with the first 5 billion the actually existing savings. The money flowed back. Then came the new bond and sucked the finances once again and with that also the remaining savings. And then the pump appeared again and sucked the billions and they again ebbed

---

20 The Erfurt Programme was the programme adopted by the Sozialdemokratische Partei Deutschlands (SPD) in 1891. It was formulated by Eduard Bernstein, August Bebel and Karl Kautsky. Kautsky (1854-1938), a Bohemian Jewish journalist, wrote the official commentary to the Erfurt programme called *Das Erfurter Programm* (1892). He considered himself an orthodox Marxist and later criticised the Bolshevik revolution and its leaders Lenin and Trotsky.

until, fortunately, after this fine game was played out nine times – the Reich had incurred debts of 100 billion.

For that the people however had finely printed paper in their hands – At first we imagined that we had become so much richer, now the state comes and says, "I am faced with bankruptcy".

But why? But I cannot myself become bankrupt when I constantly thrust my hundred mark note from my right pocket into my left. It would however be the greatest foolishness if we would further demonstrate the foolishness of our war-bond economy by declaring ourselves bankrupt.

Let us break the financial slavery to interest! Let us declare the several war-bonds, with the removal of interest, as legal currency and the nightmare of state bankruptcy will vanish from us like March snow in the sun.

I have been told that the removal of interest payment is a veiled state bankruptcy. No, that is not true! The spectre of state bankruptcy is in fact only a bogeyman of children and nurses invented by the Mammonist powers.

Fr. Röhr's book, What everybody must know about state bankruptcy, is completely ensnared in Mammonistic ways of thought, and even though the author in general clearly recognises the economic damages that threaten us through socialisation, however much and rightly he points to the fact that in the final analysis only a restructuring of our economy can save us – he cannot free himself from the superstition of the sacredness of interest and so, entirely in the interest of Mammonism, predicts state bankruptcy as a quite frightful catastrophe.

It is interesting to note that Röhr cannot free himself of that in spite of better historical knowledge and remarks in his conclusion: "If the destructive economic catastrophe is not avoided, then nobody will be spared by it", whereas on p.81 he admits that the consequences of state financial mismanagements have in part very quickly been levelled out and, on p.68, that, be that as it may, it is certain however that Russia (in the last century) overcame these currency crises without lasting disturbances.

On p.76 he says, in investigating the effects of state bankruptcy: that, of course, on the whole, far-reaching economic disturbances have emerged but that neither the destruction of the state nor that of its economic forces was thereby effected. On the contrary, a quick restoration of the state economy and a recovery of the state finances were observable. When the author then continues three lines below that state bankruptcy definitely signifies an economic catastrophe and brings about a limitless misery I am sorry that I cannot understand this logic.

But back to our special case! What is then more honest? To speak like a pharisee of the inviolability of the war-bonds and at the same time to oppress the people with an unheard of tax burden? Or, if a finance minister had the courage to appear publicly before the people and explain, "I cannot pay the interest for the war-bonds or only when I collect precisely as much in taxes from you.

… But I definitely must have had money then, during the war, a better idea did not strike me (cf. England) and so I made a swindle with war-bonds subject to high interests. Be forgiving, dear people, it was finally for you but we do not wish to hide any more – I the state pay no more interest and you tax-payers do not have to pay any taxes for the payment of these interests. That basically simplifies our businesses, we avoid the enormous tax apparatus and likewise the enormous interest-serving apparatus, thus a great amount of money and workforce".

I have refrained for a long time from the uncovering of this swindle but I consider it as absolutely essential not to lose the view of the whole for a moment.

The group of people who would bear the suffering, we mean thus those (earned income of 1500 marks) who drew more than 30,000 marks in pension capital after their tax declarations are, according to the Bavarian tax statements, 822 persons, that is only 0.4% of the tax-payers. Thus, incidentally, in the whole of Germany 10,000 (the upper 10,000!) (Bayerische Staatszeitung, 1913).

We now wish very briefly to become clear about the most important aspects of this revolutionary demand, and we wish also to consider the questions at first from the standpoint of our nation.

For this we need at first a clear view of our present situation. State Secretary Schiffer described it in his big speech in the Berlin Chamber of Commerce as "unforeseeable". That is only partly right. The enormous debt of our national economy is foreseeable, the unheard of devaluation of our currency, in short the fact that we have overnight become a poor nation.

However, the burdens which were imposed on us through the Peace Treaty are not foreseeable. The already existing debts are figured, as we have seen, at around 250 billion. Let us now assume that the Entente[21] imposes on us in some form a further 50 billion in war reparations, so that is altogether around 300 billion in debts.

However difficult it may be to squeeze them within the narrow limits of this essay, some words must still be said here on the size of the German wealth. The researches of Helfferich and Steinmann-Bucher[22] estimate the German national wealth at around 350 billion. One can ascribe to such estimates, however carefully they may have been established, only a partial value. They are valid in general only for times of undisturbed economy. But they are already even there misleading in that the state and community possessions are included as well, thus, for example, also road-constructions, stream corrections, etc. It becomes clear that the establishment of such works did indeed cost an enormous amount of money, but that they really have no intrinsic value. A better standard for the size of the national wealth is the so-called taxable wealth, as is revealed in the tax declarations for military contribution or the tax on war profits. Here there emerged a total sum of 192 billion, thus quite substantially less than according to the statement of Helfferich. To this sum may be made a further addition, based on experience, of around 10% for the legally tax-free small fortunes and a similarly large addition for "hidden assets".

In any case it appears only Utopian to speak of a national wealth of over 250 billion. But even this figure has only a quite partial worth. The most correct way would be to generally break with a national wealth that is conceivable in figures and to arrive at the knowledge that the national wealth finds its expression exclusively in the intellectual and physical workforce of the entire nation, that it belongs to a scale that has nothing to do with the narrow conception of capital. To be sure, we must also perceive another wide source of national wealth in the presence of landed properties, forests and fertile land, but even these

---

21   The Entente refers to the Allied Powers during the first world war. They
      included, in the main, the United Kingdom, France and the Russian Empire.
      The United States entered the war as an "associated power".

22   Arnold Steinmann-Bucher was the author of *Deutschlands Volksvermögen
      im Krieg,* 1919.

things cannot be conceived in terms of figures since they fluctuate between zero and infinity according as whether the landed properties lie fallow or are valued on the basis of geological surveys at billions of tons of coal, etc.

We do not wish to forget that Germany is actually a poor country. It possesses almost no monopolies. In landed wealth it stands far behind most of the neighbouring countries, not to mention the untold landed wealth of the Chinese, Indian and American empires. In fertility of land it stands far behind the blessed domains of the Russian black earth, the effortlessly producing tropical and subtropical stretches of land. So in the final analysis there remains to us only the workforce and the will to work of our people as well as the presence of sufficient work and we must be clear on the fact that in this matter of funded loans one cannot speak of a real security for our debts.

Whether interest-bearing war-bonds or non-interest-bearing Reich banknotes, there stands behind them only the driving force of the entire population, and what is the driving force but a function of the work performance of the entire working population.

We must be clear briefly about yet another node of questions that is broached here and that is about the main items of our state revenue sources and expenses. There is a remarkable contradiction between the wide space that the question of money raising assumes in our private life and the interest that we allot to the big questions of the financial conduct of our state, and yet indeed there exists no essential difference between individual economy and national economy.

The main items of the state revenues are: first, the net proceeds of the post and railways, second, those from mines, forest commissions and other state enterprises, thirdly, the customs and indirect taxes, and fourth, the direct taxes.

In order not to provide merely theoretical statements in the case of such eminently practical questions, I wish to briefly explain, in the case of the Bavarian state budget[23] of 1911, the individual items

---

23   The following data on the Bavarian state budget are taken in rounded figures from the Bavarian State Yearbook of 1913. This is the last statistical yearbook that appeared before the war that gives comprehensive information on the Bavarian finances. No new editions appeared during the war ...

according to their order of magnitude. Post, telegraph and railways[24] brought 120 million, forests, mines, etc. around 40 million, indirect taxes 53 million, direct taxes 60 million. A further 67 million flowed from stamp duties, fees, inheritance taxes, property benefits, transfers on the part of the Reich, etc.

Now how is it with the expenses? We find here, in the first place, the expenses for the interest of the state debt, including the railway bonds, at 85 million. For the royal house 5 million, administration of justice 27 million, internal administration 40 million, churches and schools 51 million, financial administration 13 million, expenses for state goals 50 million, pensions 36 million, sundry expenses 5 million. The annual budget then showed a revenue surplus of 27 million in this fortunate year of Bavarian finances.

However, within the scope of our thought only the expenses that can be cancelled through the breaking of interest slavery interest us. Here naturally stands in the first place the expense for the interest payment of the state debt at 85 million, and, in addition, most part of our expense for the financial administration at some 10 million, then a great part of the expenses for state goals, a half of which we wish to register at 25 million and, finally, the expenses for the royal house at 5 million are today cancelled, altogether 125 million.

The absence of these items means the possibility of dispensing with the raising of all direct and indirect taxes which, as we saw, brought in 53 and 60, 113 million in all! Now we are not at all of the opinion that one should entirely eliminate the direct and indirect taxes, within reasonable limits they doubtlessly operate on the one hand in an educational manner, on the other in a regulating one. It is certainly no longer right and proper that the income from funded property remain subject to a moderate, staggered tax; the state must indeed also, with its instruments of power, provide for undisturbed property; it seems equally advisable that trade and industry be held liable to corresponding tax payments from their entrepreneurial profits, for them the state has to

---

24   The unprecedented rise of wage rates and material prices led to the fact that the net proceeds of the Bavarian state railways sank in 1913 to 3 million marks compared to on average 80 million marks in the previous years. In Prussia, according to the reports of the Finance Minister Simon, there even appeared, instead of the proceeds up to now of, on average, 700 million marks, a deficit of 1,300,000,000. So we are able less than ever to think of a sudden raising of the direct and indirect taxes; we must more than ever think of removing the new debts arisen through catastrophic financial economy through entirely forceful confiscation of wealth, especially very large wealth.

take care of the maintenance and construction of public thoroughfares; a corresponding minimum poll tax for every enfranchised citizen is likewise a just demand, and the responsibility for security of the individual and property is also demanded of the state.

In the field of indirect taxes, a powerful dismantling of all purely luxury taxes could work in a regulating way in the best sense whereas all the pure food items and requirements of the nation are to be held free of taxes!

The result of such a tax policy would have to be sought less in the high financial result – of that there can be no question since, for the great mass of the population, it should be not a real tax burden but only a reminder that man is not only an individual but also a state citizen and has, besides state citizens' rights, also state citizens' duties. The profits should be used less for the relief of the commercial state companies whose pure profits, as we have seen, suffice to defray the ordinary expenses of the state for education, development, administration of justice, internal administration, etc. They should be used to promote such cultural tasks of the state for which there were never corresponding means at disposal within the scope of the ordinary state budget. I think here in the first place of nurseries, institutions for the blind and crippled, crèches, maternity leave, the fight against tuberculosis, against alcoholic and venereal diseases, for the construction of garden cities and settlements, especially for the accommodation and humane care of our war wounded.

Our view is broadened. We glimpse a new land. Could the breaking of interest slavery mean the abolition of all taxes? It would mean that if we had emerged from this gigantic war as a victorious nation. So we do not wish to exult too soon; the burdens placed on us by our enemies will take care of that. But still we glimpse a new land on the basis of the observation just made, and indeed one that is most simple, of our Bavarian state budget.

Essentially we find quite similar relations in the other German federal states and it is not an exaggeration to say that, from the surpluses of the commercial state enterprises, that is, the railways, post, telegraph, forests, mines, etc., all state expenses for the entire state administration of justice, for the entire internal administration, including state buildings, all expenses for education and development, as well as for religious purposes, can be financed without any difficulty. Thus a really ideal situation.

Why is it not so? Interest has crept in. On account of the payment of interest, food is made costlier for the population, on account of interest, sugar and salt, beer and wine, matches and tobacco, and numberless other requirements of daily need are burdened with indirect taxes. On account of the interests, one must raise the direct taxes which are divided into land taxes, which are shifted onto raised corn prices, property taxes which drive the rents up, commercial taxes which burden the productive work, income taxes which cannot be shaken off and depress the standard of living of civil servants and those with fixed incomes, and finally, at the very end, modest in its gifts, insatiable in its receipts, comes loan capital with taxes on capital pensions. According to the tax declarations of 1911, out of 253 million matured capital pensions received, a total of 8.1 million was paid to state taxes.

We have seen that every capital pension, every capital interest must, in the final analysis, be raised exclusively through the work of the entire population. We have seen that the interest payment for the state debts makes up the biggest item in our state budget, and we have seen that the capital pension taxpayers contribute only a very modest share to the state revenues.

With 8 million of the total sum of direct taxes of 60 million, the capitalist pays proportionally only an eighth or sixth of the direct taxes in Bavaria in 1911. The direct taxes are proportionally roughly a fifth of the entire state revenues. Therewith loan capital makes a grant of only a 30th or 48th of the entire state needs.

It cannot be denied that the tax legislation in the last years, especially during the war, entered into a strong dependence on capital pensions, but the stronger indirect taxation went almost in tandem with it so that the proportion was hardly altered.

The picture becomes horrible only when we consider our Reich budget. Here the relations are in themselves already much more unfavourable. The Reich does not have the tax sources that the individual federal states do. The direct taxes are reserved for the federal states, the commercial enterprises of the Reich are limited to the Reich post and the Reich railways (thus, N.B., without the Prussian state railways!) and therewith remain only the customs and indirect taxes.

The dimensions of these Reich income sources (see the State Yearbook for the German Reich of 1917 and 1918) were, in 1915: 1 billion Reich post and railways, 0.7 billion customs, 1 billion indirect taxes, 0.8

billion special incomes (war contribution, levy contributions[25]), etc. Here too again the same picture. More than a third, that is 1.3 billion, was gobbled up in 1915 by the interest of the Reich debt. Even here the loan capital forced itself in once again. Even here all the indirect taxes rise to satisfy it. Sugar pays 163 million, salt 61 million, beer 128 million, tobacco, brandy, champagne, lamps, matches, playing cards, and countless other taxable sources have to pay to scrape up a billion, which then flows fully into the pockets of the capitalists.

Today the raising of the debt interests of the Reich are alone a mystery. Indeed, the interests on our 100 billion war bonds, as well as on the other war credits alone consume 8 billion. The revenues from the post and railways can hardly be raised. We could hardly raise the customs, so there remains only a raising of the indirect taxes five or ten times; an impossibility! or the clear insight that only the breaking of the financial slavery to interest can bring deliverance. The entire war bond economy was an enormous self-deception. The German nation borrowed from itself hundred billion for its war. It promised for it 5 billion in interest; so it has to pay 5 billion in taxes. Only the big capitalist has a profit who receives so many capital pensions that he cannot possibly spend them and, as we have seen, only a very small percentage is indeed taken away from him.

I hope that, through the broad strokes of my argumentation, I have banished the humanly conceivable alarm of many readers regarding the possible loss of interest receipts from their fine securities. An example may be pointed to just very briefly that the entire interest economy is a great self-deception and I wish to push thereby the upper limit of the earning capacity of good citizens.

Given the case that the work income of the head of a family is 10,000 marks and, in addition to that, 5000 marks from capital pensions, there are from these at first around 1500 marks of direct taxes to be paid, and further at least 1000 marks must be deducted in the form of costly rents; a further 1000 marks may be consumed by the indirect taxes of the five- to six-member family, and now one recognises that already of the happy tax relations of earlier years of the fine capital pensions of the small and medium capitalists not much indeed remains. Already today one can no longer speak of "remaining" at all; on the contrary, substantial parts of the work income will perhaps be further taken away when one examines the fantastic present-day tax plans.

---

25   [Levies that federal states pay to the Reich towards war expenses.]

Naturally the matter looks quite different for the big capitalist who, let us say, receives only 1 million in capital pensions. (There are today rather many of such people in Germany). This lucky man pays in capital taxes, when it is high, 50-60,000 marks. In indirect taxes too he does not pay more than the family head of the previous example. For the maintenance of his household he can still live quite pleasantly in the end, even in the present expensive times, with 40-50,000 marks. There remain for him only around 900,000 marks net, for which he will receive in the following year, at 5% interest, a further 45,000 marks, and that legally, at the expense of the working population.

The small pensioner who lives only on his interests would doubtlessly be harmed. If he is able-bodied, he must naturally decide to obtain a work income. With it he then still sets himself up very much better than the millions of his national comrades who have nothing apart from their physical or intellectual working power. If he does not wish that, he must use up his wealth. For 20 years he has to keep drawing from it if, he consumes from now on, as up to now, a 5% interest. For persons who are not in a position to work or are debilitated by illness or age care must be provided with a suitable existence through the development of social welfare for all circles of the population. I imagine social welfare as follows:

Let us suppose that an elderly woman, a widow, who up to now had to live on the interests of capital assets of 60,000 marks is, through the legally announced breaking of interest slavery, robbed of her source of income. Here, through the widest expansion of the system of life annuities, an opportunity would be given to the person in question to receive a life pension corresponding to her capital, whereby the yearly pension could even be raised with regard to the interest proceeds up to now in order to give a certain compensation for the reduced monetary value. Thus, in such a way that, for example, for the supplied 60,000 marks in debt instruments of the Reich or the state or in bond certificates, a yearly life-long annuity of 40,000 marks could be given. If the widow has children and if she wishes to bequeath a part of her wealth to them, it may be allowed to her to transform only 40,000 marks into a life-annuity while the remaining 20,000 marks remain preserved for the children. Out of the 40,000 marks, up to 1/12th of the supplied capital could be given, according to the age of the one seeking the life-annuity. Even here it should be pointed out again that through the breaking of interest slavery the living costs of the widow are made quite substantially cheaper through the discontinuation of the oppressive taxes.

It would go far beyond the scope of this essay to go in detail into the personal interests of individual strata of the population. In the case of such a revolutionary demand it can also not be a question of personal interests and yet, in the development of the idea, one will find that the salutary consequences will finally personally benefit every individual.

Precisely in the problem broached already above, of the freeing of the war bonds from interest, I have already attempted to make clear that the small capitalist, that is, all the hundred thousand who, through a more than American advertising activity for the war bond scheme, were induced to an investment of their savings, have not only nothing of the interests because they indeed have to pay the taxes for them by themselves but must, in the case of the tax legislation geared to the preservation of large capital, pay for the interests of the subscriptions of millions. I think that, apart from these very real observations, just an appeal to all bond-holders concerned about the welfare of their children should suffice to accept the waiver of eternal interest from the debts of the Reich as entirely natural. What then, in this case, does the patriot lose who gave his fatherland in its greatest need 10,000 marks other than just a usurious claim to receive 50,000 marks in interests alone within hundred years, without the capital thereby having worn off in the least? His children and grandchildren must work eternally so that just these interests may first of all be paid off.

The question of the return payment of lent sums can be resolved in different ways. In my brief thoughts on the problems at hand that I submitted to the government of the People's Republic of Bavaria[26] on 20 November before someone, I made the suggestion of effecting, in place of interest payment, return payment in 20 annual instalments of 5%. I think I may be able to make in the following another far better suggestion which, on account of its simplicity, certainly deserves to be preferred: "The war-bond instruments are, on the abolition of interest, declared to be legal currency". That is the Columbus egg. The advantage of this measure is, first, that really nobody notices anything of it. The loan instruments remain lying quietly in the deposits, only they do not have any children, as little as a book or a cupboard, or any other usable object that one has loaned to one's friend.

---

26   [The Bavarian Soviet Republic was established in April 1919, although Bavaria was declared to be a "free" state already in November 1918 by the Jewish socialist Kurt Eisner, who was assassinated in February 1919. The loyalists of the German national army and the Freikorps defeated the Communists who led the Republic, in street battles, in May 1919.]

If one needs money, one gets hold of a war-bond certificate and pays with it. The war-bond certificates also have, after all, as much beauty and paper value as our other 10-, 20-,100- and 1000 mark notes. There cannot at all be a question of a flooding of the market with currencies in the case of such a smooth transformation of the interest economy into an interest-free economy. The war-bonds are indeed already fully preserved and saved in the bank treasuries or other stashes considered by the people as more theft-free than a stocking or a rubbish heap. Indeed, the fact cannot be denied that the paper currencies that are spent to a sum of roughly 40 billion are not in circulation but are, for the most part, stored in the ways described above. Our currency requirement was, even during the times of the economic boom before the war, only around 4 - 6 billion and there can be no question that today, with increasingly accepted cash-free payment transactions, we would need more than double this sum.

The removal of interest for all fixed-interest stocks is obviously to be carried out in an exactly similar way. For these stocks, as well as for the dividends, however, the "repayment" in 20 or 25 instalments that was originally planned for all shares will be more advisable. The breaking of the interest slavery in the case of mortgages doubtless signifies the solution of the housing problem, the liberation from exorbitant rents. It is as little understandable why the owner of a mortgage should have an endless enjoyment of interest from a sum that was loaned once, why an effortless and endless flow of goods should be granted to him, why the great mass of the people should pay year in year out high rents just for the sake of this unhealthy interest principle. Let it be very briefly indicated that naturally there can be no question of a full abolition of rent since the administration and maintenance of houses constantly demands work and money. So there can emerge a lowering of rents only insofar as it is brought about through the successful repayment of mortgages.

One thing alone should be emphasised quite sharply, that the breaking of interest slavery does not have the least in common with our entire value-producing work insofar as in no way is any impediment prepared for the entrepreneurial spirit, productive work, the production of goods, the acquisition of wealth; on the contrary, the entire working population is, as we have seen, liberated from a gloomy, mysterious, heavy burden; our spiritual life is purged of an intoxicating poison.

How correctly the proliferation of the interest problem has been recognised in the course of history we perceive from the fact that the interest problem has occupied minds at all times and in all nations.

In the Old Testament we find in many passages, for example, 3 Moses 25,[27] 5 Moses 15,[28] stipulations on interest reductions in the form that the seventh year should always be a year of quiet or a jubilee year in which all the debts of national comrades should be dropped.

In 594 B.C., Solon abolished by law the slavery to personal debt. This law was called the great Seisachtheia (the casting off of burdens).

In ancient Rome, the Lex Gemicia of 332 B.C. summarily forbade Roman citizens to take interest.

Under Justinian a prohibition of interest was decreed with the stipulation that generally no interests should be demanded any longer if the interest arrears have grown to the amount of the original loaned capital.

Pope Leo I the Great decreed in 443 a universal prohibition against taking interest; it was up to then forbidden only to clerics to demand interest on a loan. Now the prohibition of interest became part of the canonical law and also a rule binding on laymen. Gradually even the secular legislation adopted the canonical views and even threatened interest taking with punishment. We find this in the Reich's police ordinances of 1500, 1530 and 1577.

To be sure, such laws were much contested and evaded on many occasions and it may be mentioned further in this very brief historical review as an astonishing historical fact that, whereas the canonical law had from the 11th to the 17th century forbidden interest taking to Christians, this had been permitted to the Jews.

It would be extraordinarily pleasing to investigate what negative economic phenomena led in the meantime to this powerful lifting of burdens. It would be especially valuable to see what powers and forces the prohibitions of interest broke through.

Indeed, in the Middle Ages, short shrift was often made of usurers, the peasants or the citizens who had been sucked dry got together and killed the usurers. Today we have entered a quite different developmental stage of the interest problem. Such pogroms are deeply condemned. And it is also no longer a question of individual locally

---

27   [Leviticus 25.]

28   [Deuteronomy 15.]

limited manifestations of a sickness that could be combated through the removal of the suppurative core, it is a matter of a serious illness of the whole of mankind. It may be stressed quite especially that precisely our present-day culture, the internationalism of economic relations, makes the interest principle so deadly. The historical review that was given may also not be an analogy for the present-day relations. When the Babylonians overcame the Assyrians, the Romans the Carthaginians, the Germans the Romans, there was no continuance of interest slavery; there were no international world-powers. Wars were also not financed by loans but with the treasuries collected during peace. David Hume gives a very fine summary of it in his essay on state credit.[29] Only the modern age with its continuity of possession and its international law allowed loan capitals to rise immeasurably. The penny that was placed on interest at the time of the birth of Christ does not exist any more, since all property rights of authority had to yield many times in the intervening period; on the other hand, there exists the penny that the old Rothschild placed on interest and will, if there is an international law, exist forever. One must besides consider that wide stretches of the earth moved only in the modern age from a natural economy to a financial economy. In this context it is very important that only in the middle of the previous century were all limits on interest-taking or interest prohibitions removed. In this way in England in 1854, in Denmark in 1856, in Belgium in 1865, in Austria in 1868.

So not much older than a half century is the conception of interest that is today considered inseparable from financial property. But precisely this conception of interest first allowed money to become the demoniacal authority with such universal power that we have come to know. The debt of states – at first incipient and then becoming ever stronger - with regard to the capitalist dates from only the middle of the past century. Only from this time do we see the state sink from custodian of the community of the people to the custodian of capitalist interests. This development reached its high point in the war-bonds which we meet in all countries that, as we have seen, exclusively serve only Mammonistic interests and on which the crown will now be placed in the form of the gigantic credit structure of an international loan.

These brief reviews may make it easier for us to finally break with

---

29   [David Hume (1711-1776) was a Scottish empiricist and anti-rationalist. His essay "Of Public Credit" was published in his *Political Discourses,* 1752]

the idea that to loan capital should be given the supernatural power to grow from itself eternally and unstoppably. Endowed with a frightful sucking power. We must break with the idea that loan capital should be able to be enthroned above the clouds untouched by world happenings and disappearances, untouched by the past, untouched by the powers of destruction, untouched by the bullets of our gigantic guns. For even if houses and cottages, railways and bridges shattered by grenades sink into dust and ashes, the mortgages remain standing, the railway and state debts are not destroyed by it. If villages and cities, entire provinces fall victim to the senseless destruction of war, what does it matter to it, this means new debts. With eyes glowing with greed the Golden International enthroned above the clouds watches the wild activities of mankind. And the time is not far when finally all of mankind without exception will serve Mammonism as interest slaves ...

The idea is international; it must liberate the entire world. Glory to the nation that first dares the daring step. Soon all the others will follow. The question often posed to me if the idea is in general realisable nationally I answer with "yes". We are internally in debt. At present we are naturally powerless against foreign interest claims; they must indeed be paid. Excessive capital drain must be stopped but, as little as the legislator refrains from developing laws against murder, manslaughter, fraud, etc. because there would always be wretched people, so little may a nation as a whole refrain from taking a step recognised as necessary for the healing of its state finances simply because not precisely the best sections of the people try to transfer their collected money to safety abroad. Assuming that hundreds, nay thousands of millions of war bonds would be taken abroad, yet even this could not be a decisive factor for the neglect of the breaking of interest slavery, for proportionately the greatest part of the 250 billion fixed-interest internal assets must remain at home.

We would like to sum up in brief once again. The breaking of interest slavery is the radical means for the final and lasting healing of our state finances. The breaking of interest slavery means the possibility of abandoning oppressive direct and indirect taxes since the commercial enterprises of the state have up to now already, and ever more after the control of further fields suited for socialising (inland shipping, electricity supply, air traffic, etc.), been supplying sufficient surpluses to the state treasuries to defray therefrom all social and cultural tasks of the state.

Beyond this financial point of view, the breaking of the interest slavery of productive work in all professional fields will grant it the primary position due to it. Money will once again be returned to its sole appropriate role of being a servant in the enormous enterprise of our national economy. It will become once again what it is, an indication of performed work and therewith the way will be paved to a higher goal, the rejection of the frenzied financial greed of our age.

This idea wishes to establish a tightly formed front of the entire working population, from the unpropertied worker who, as we have seen, is used very powerfully by way of indirect taxes for the satisfaction of loan capital, to the entire bourgeois section of officials and salaried workers, of the peasant and small business middle class, who feel the ruthless tyranny of money in the form of accommodation distress, land interests, bank interests, etc., and, much farther, to the leading figures, inventors and directors of our big industry, who, one and all, are stuck more or less in the talons of big loan capital, for whom their first life's task is always: to acquire pensions, interests, dividends, for the financial powers acting behind the corridors. No less belong to this also all the circles of the intelligentsia, artists, authors, actors, scientists, as well the others belonging to free professions.

If consciously or instinctively big loan capital, as a group of persons or as a personification of the interest principle, seeks to conceal the fact of its unlimited ambition to rule, if our entire jurisdiction hitherto serving Roman law, thus a law serving the protection of a plutocracy, has forced the protection of property into the foreground and therewith penetrated the legal consciousness of our people, the breaking of the financial slavery to interest must come as the only way out of the threatening economic enslavement of the entire world through the Golden International, as one of the ways of throwing out the poison of Mammonism with its corruption and contamination of the mentality of our age.

The Conversion Of War-Bonds Into Bank Assets

The transformation of war-bonds, etc. into legal currency demanded in Art.1[30] has brought forth repeatedly the objection of the excessive flooding of the market with currencies. This objection is indeed in

---

30   [See above p.13]

itself quite erroneous. The inflation exists through the mere existence of war-bonds. But it is true that the thought of the physical existence of these instruments transformed into currency will not, in spite of its erroneousness, be quietened and therefore, in spite of its unreality, may lead to unfavourable offshoots as if in fact a new inflation had taken place; so we demand, through a change of Art.1, the conversion of war-bonds as well as the other state debts, under a legal abolition of interest, into bank assets.

This formulation has the great advantage that the apparent form of war-bonds as securities would disappear, the war-bond instruments would have to be delivered to the Reich bank by the banks, bankers, savings banks, etc. and will, against credit notes of equivalent value, be destroyed. Therewith would almost every man in Germany receive a bank asset, an open bank account which he can avail of.

Such a dealing would have, besides, also the great advantage that a withholding of big assets in private possession would not be possible since, after the expiration of a certain time-limit, the war-bonds that are not delivered would be considered invalid. Besides, a check would still be possible of how many war-bonds have been taken abroad. The last point however cannot in any way hinder the execution of the breaking of interest slavery for, if we feel really too weak in comparison to foreign countries, then we must just satisfy the interest demands coming from abroad, but I am personally fully of the opinion that we must maintain the interest free declaration even with regard to foreign loan possessions. We need not expect that, in the case of such a course of action which resembles a reawakening self-consciousness, the foreign interest claims would be carried out with the force of arms, for, in fact, in history never yet has a warlike action been undertaken against a large state on account of financial measures in favour of private persons. It also need not be imagined that indeed the French nation, on account of the interest claims of Messrs. Mayer, Schulze and Cohn from Germany based on their German war-bonds brought with them over the border, would set an ultimatum to Germany.

It would moreover be possible, indeed in order to avoid the appearance of a state bankruptcy in front of foreign countries, to carry out a lottery of the war-bonds which could then indeed, on the basis of the obligatory delivery to the winning numbers, be easily established in such a way that even the numbers that are to be accepted abroad would be first picked out and paid in Reich banknotes. A third would be the welcome declaration of the distribution of the war-bonds and the accompanying possibility of an extraordinarily simple tax collection of wealth tax in that the rent officers would only need to instruct the Reich bank offices to lay on the account of Mr. X a tax of so many marks. In this way the payment of taxes would be much more painless – naturally the veto power of the tax-payers would remain in its full scope.

In the case of such a transformation (conversion) of the war-bonds into bank assets, a certain social levelling too could be effected insofar as small items of war-bonds - thus all small subscriptions of all those people to whom the subscription of a war-bond is really to be reckoned as a patriotic act, so, let us say, up to 5,000 or 10,000 marks - would be valued at par while all greater subscriptions could be valued at the current rate. The credit items for all the other state instruments would have to be treated in entirely the same way.

Special Explanations of the Legal Demand in the Manifesto

To Art.1 - It is quite essential that all state and communal debts be treated in the same way since only in this way can a uniform broad regulation of our entire financial system be carried out along with the breaking of interest slavery.

To Art.2 -That the breaking of interest slavery must be undertaken simultaneously in the case of all other fixed-interest instruments is already clear from the principle, in order not to cause a senseless rocketing of these instruments; this would then obviously occur if the state instruments were just declared to be interest-free. The removal of the debt as such would have to be effected through an annual repayment whereby a constant and uniform relief of all debt-charged objects would be brought about.

To Art.3 – This clause stands in closest connection with the above as well as with the nationalisation of real-estate credit demanded in art.5. The peasant or house-owner burdened with mortgages continues to pay before and after the amount that he had to pay the creditor up to now but no longer as eternal interest but as repayment. After 20, 25 or 30 years, according to the level of the interest rate up to now, the land and house property will be freed of debt. The mortgage bank for its part can naturally likewise continue to pay the bond certificate owners according to the bond certificates only during this time. Hand in hand with this relief there appears: the right of the community to the possession of real assets freed from mortgages.

First of all must come a general housing or real-estate land registry, for even the debt-free land ownership naturally has the right to repayment of the invested capital as well as a lasting claim to a part of the rent for the defraying of all the expenses, charges, etc. bound to land ownership as well as to a corresponding compensation for personal pains.

We would like to explain this in general outlines in the description of a city apartment building. The building has a value of 100,000 marks. Thereof is recorded first the debt claim of 50,000 marks at 4% of a mortgage bank, second of 20,000 marks at 5% from the private sector, and 30,000 marks is made up by the money brought by the building owner himself. The rent receipts are 7000 marks. From this is to be paid for the first mortgage 2000 marks, for the second mortgage 1000 marks, for charges, expenses, etc. 1000 marks, in total 4000 marks. There remains therewith for the building owner 3000 marks as interest yield for his own expended capital of 30,000 marks.

After implementation of the legal abolition of interest on money, the situation after 10 years is the following: 1st mortgage 30,000 marks, 2nd mortgage 20,000 marks. The capital requirement of the building owner is entirely repaid, on the other hand a new state property right has emerged to the sum of 50,000 marks. Therewith there begins for the state a right to co-determination on further rent receipts, as well on as the fixing of rent prices. Now it would be unjust to equate the building owner, as regards repayment, with the mortgages. For his capital is not in the narrow sense the pure loan capital that has to be hit with the breaking of interest slavery; here it is a matter of "risk capital", that is, money transformed into a valuable property, that is, a building. Therefore either a long period of rent income or a corresponding percentage from the charges of the building is to be granted to the building owner.

It cannot be our task to make in this place any binding plans; it is only a matter of suggestions, of stimulations, that like a smooth transformation of interest economy into an interest-free economy could succeed even in the field of land ownership. In order to complete the example further, let us suppose the situation after 25 years: then all mortgages are repaid, only the lasting expenses are the same or, on account of the high age of the building, raised from 1000 marks to, for example, 1,500 marks. The rate granted to the building owner from this sum would also be around 1000 to 1500 marks, then the picture emerges that around 3000 marks of the rent receipts are actually lasting burdens whereas the surplus 4000 marks of the original 7000 marks would be freely disposable. The state therefore has the ability to reduce the rents by more than half; it will do this, for example, in workers' houses or it reduces it only around 20-, 30- or 40% and acquires from the difference remaining over an enormous revenue source for other state requirements, first of all naturally for the new construction of accommodation to be carried out by the state. In mansions the rents will not be reduced, or much reduced, from which further very large resources will be made available also for the better construction of accommodation or for special social purposes. This future fact however opens – and I consider that as a very promising prospect – the inner justification for the community (state) to intervene already now in the determination of rent prices in the manner outlined by me above of a reduction of the rent prices of the workers' houses; in the growing claim of the state to land ownership lies the foundation of a well-founded central bank, the issuance of credit against mortgage creditors.

To Art.4 and 5 - These clauses demand the socialising of the entire financial system. Money is only and exclusively the recognition given by a state community of performed work. The issuance of money bills is one of the sovereign basic rights of the state. The falsification of state money bills stands under the severest penalty, so it is a downright urgent social requirement that the financial system be placed under the control of the whole. The work performance of the whole is the sole basis of money bills and only the failure to recognise this basic fact has led to the neglect of our state finances and to the complete anarchy of the financial system in general.

With the transfer of personal and commercial loans to private bankers suggested in Art.5 a deep cut is made into the entire financial system. For the state credit system as well as for the communal and also for real-estate credit, one should adhere to the breaking of interest slavery with the most extreme consistency and energy because it is in general the indispensable precondition for the social state.

It is different with personal credit. In and of itself we place on personal credit too the demand of interest abolition but to this demand is no longer attached the enormous and principal significance. We remember the 250 billion fixed-interest loan capital compared to the mere 12 billion equity instruments. All such credits, stocks, share

44

certificates, participating interests, etc. are risk capital. The proceeds from these capitals depend on the diligence and efficiency of those persons to whom the money has been entrusted. So here there enters into the question the factor of risk, of the danger of loss, as well as of personal trust. So a certain compensation of a special sort still seems essential. The owner of shares, etc. does not receive any compensation or profit when the enterprise to which he has entrusted his money does not earn anything. He loses all his money if the enterprises collapses. It is different, for example, in the case of the holder of the debts of the Reich railways. The Reich railways lost completely with the loss of Elsaß-Lothringen. Nevertheless the owner of railway bonds continues to receive his interests. From whom? From the taxes of all. Even if the railways work with as great an adverse balance as in Prussia and Bavaria in the last years, the bond holders receive their interests nevertheless. From whom? From the customs duty from the workforce and the consumption of the working population.

One may understand just this basic difference – in order to finally recognise where the vampire sucks on the workforce of the people. So personal credit should remain assigned or directed once again to personal treatment by the private bank. The personal efficiency of loan-seekers which the banker is personally aware of should once again become decisive for personal credit. The fees determined by the state regulate themselves according to the availability of money that already comes into being through the breaking of interest slavery.

To Art.6 – That which was said in principle in Art.5 is valid also for dividends in particular. In the interest of the social state community it should meanwhile be demanded that, even for the large industrial enterprises, a repayment of the once loaned capital should be aimed at – in order to introduce even here an abolition of the debt of the individual industrial works to those that are only investors. For in fact is repeated here on a smaller scale what we were able to observe in the case of large loan capital with regard to entire populations. Even here the capitalist exploits the worker, the foreman, the engineer, the entrepreneur quite in the same way, for the pressure to earn dividends comes first. If however we reach the status of industrial and commercial enterprises freed from the vampire of eternal interest, only then is the way open to the reduction of prices, manufacture, the appropriation and distribution of surplus value, partly to the community partly to the workers and officials and the directorate of the individual enterprises, thus to those who alone actually create the production of goods and values.

To Art.7 – In this clause is involved naturally also the entire domain of the insurance system that can be built up analogously on an interest-free basis. The premiums paid cannot grow through the addition of interests, but the insurance companies become savings banks, that is, the insurance risk and the insurance advantage remain preserved. For this the state community has to compensate.

To Art.8 – With reference to the devaluation of our money, which came about only through the enormous mass of our innumerable state debts, we demand a strongly graded wealth tax. In this we place the emphasis on "strongly graded". For a wealth tax, a stamping of notes, etc., is now also nothing but a self-deception with which sand is thrown in one's eyes. For if I also confiscate everywhere a half of all the wealth and let it be paid in security papers, and destroy these, thereby only securities become rarer and as a result of that the conversion factor receives a fictive value raised to the same degree. Only the consumable goods and commodities always have a real value, never the paper recognitions of performed work. Another question is whether therewith the currency rate of our mark standard can be improved. But even this improvement of the currency rate is once again, in the final analysis, dependent only on the workforce and production, that is, on the productive capacity of our entire national economy.

The Objections And Their Refutation

Never has an idea been able to be carried through without contradiction, at least an idea that breaks so radically with the views formerly brought forward of the sanctity and inviolability of interest. In the objections raised and to be expected there are always two things to be observed; first is to be investigated: What is an intended distortion of the idea of the breaking of interest slavery in the objections made and, second, What is to be answered to all honest and objective doubts.

The most common objection is the claim that without the enjoyment of interest nobody will loan his money.

We indeed do not wish any more that anybody loan his money. Credit was the trick, the trap into which our entire economy entered and in which it is now so helplessly enmeshed. If the people need more capital really urgently, they get the necessary monies interest-free only against repayment to the central state bank, possibly it will issue new banknotes - why then should it issue interest-bearing notes?! - it is the same whether it is interest-bearing or interest-free paper! - behind it stands only the workforce, the tax-paying capacity of the people. Why burden from the start every state expense with the lead-weight of eternal interest?

Yes, but, how should the state fulfil its cultural works in relation to the whole? It must surely have money and can fulfil this task only by way of loan against interest.

This claim is based on an exclusively Mammonistic thought process. According to a fundamental reading of the manifesto it is definitely considered as deception, for we have, first, proved that all cultural and social tasks of the state can, after the breaking of interest slavery, be readily backed by the commercial state enterprises, the revenues of the post, railways, mines, forests, etc. Second, it is the responsibility of every sovereign state to take care of special cultural tasks through the issuance of interest-free stamps instead of the interest-bearing securities declared to be the rule in the Mammonistic state. It is not at all apparent why the state should raise the cost of special cultural tasks, for example, construction of railways, canals and hydroelectric plants through a promise of eternal interest. If it cannot pay the construction costs, etc. out of the circulating currency of its commercial state enterprises, there is no reason why the state should not make the money, a sovereign people should indeed pay for it since it acknowledges this money as currency. But why should a people with its entire workforce and taxable capacity place itself behind another piece of paper (the interest-bearing loan) that imposes an eternal interest-obligation on the people as a whole for the benefit of the capitalist? So, out with this fixed idea of the Mammonistic state.

The capitalists will then gather the expended paper instruments to themselves and hoard paper money.

Two things go against that. First, then the demand would indeed be already automatically fulfilled that mere possession of money should be unproductive, and the breaking of interest slavery voluntarily accepted by the capitalists; for, if the capitalist stores up his paper money at home, he naturally forfeits interests. Second, there goes against it the anxiety of the capitalist about his money, one need only imagine the sleepless nights of the hoarder of paper money who has large amounts of money stored up at home and who must see his possession constantly threatened by thieves, robbers, burglars, house searches, fire and flooding. I am convinced that a man of the petty bourgeoisie would not cope for long with these tensions and would soon find his way to the bank. The state bank issues a voucher and is responsible for the holdings but not for any interests. Besides, there still remains open to every man a third possibility, that is, to work with his money, to create value and produce goods, to participate in industrial undertakings, to make his life ever richer and finer, to support art and science, in short, to utilise his money in a beneficial way through a rejection of Mammonism.

But it can be that for some purposes urgent need of private capital may occur, for example, for the testing of inventions, establishment of businesses by young, industrious craftsmen, business people, etc.

First of all, this has nothing at all to do with the breaking of interest slavery! For, first, one must logically suppose that the capitalist who indeed does not, after the breaking of interest slavery, have any more opportunity to place his money absolutely safely and speculate on indolent enjoyment of interest will be inclined much more than before to risk his money on such purposes, that therefore a lack or need in this direction will occur much less than before, or has one not, quite the contrary, heard over and over again from the most efficient business people, from the cleverest inventors the complaint about how hard it is to obtain money for such purposes in the Mammonistic state if a "pension" could not be guaranteed for it? Secondly, it must be the task of the coming state to help forward every industrious force through generous support. In the old bureaucratic state also there were already attempts at this in the past, but so petty that mostly, instead of a promotion, there was brought about a restriction and frustration through the vexatious conditions connected with the granting of state support. Third, it should be noted that with the granting of several millions very much could be achieved. The willingness to work, industry and tenacity of the German inventor, engineer, craftsman, etc. is so great that, through the state's participation right in the results of successful inventions, the expenses incurred would most probably be abundantly recovered. (England as an example).

The breaking of interest slavery necessarily leads to the depletion of wealth.

Oh! Who says that? Or perhaps yes! One who has set his life on the consumption of his capital interests and cannot decide to work, for him that is certainly right; he will in 20 years, with an annual 5% consumption, be totally finished with his wealth. But that is indeed completely in order. We indeed desire the breaking of interest slavery, we wish that capital pension ceases to be the highest ideal for the state citizen. We wish to stop with this Mammonistic corruption, we do not wish to tolerate any longer that a man, that many, can live for long comfortably merely on their interests, that is, at the cost of others.

I return: it is also not at all true that the breaking of interest would lead to the abolition and depletion of wealth. On the contrary, the breaking of interest slavery promotes the building of wealth on the basis of work that has been freed from eternal interest expenses, and that is unburdened, value creating and productive of goods. The breaking of interest leads, as we have seen, to a radical lowering of the cost of life as a whole, it frees us from the excessive tax pressure so that for every working man the possibility of making savings must in future be greater than up to now. One more thing! The economic work producing goods and values of industry, trade and the professions will indeed not in any way be restricted by the breaking of interest slavery but, on the contrary, be promoted as much as possible.

What is the benefit to the worker if the capitalists do not receive any more interest?

This question should not really have arisen any more! First, it was the constant battle-cry of the workers that the capitalists would exploit the workers, secondly, we have clearly seen that precisely the worker is liable for the payment, in the form of indirect taxes, of the loan interests, see p.40.

The family bonds are weakened and torn if one cannot leave the children any wealth.

So, how does it stand here? Quite generally I think that money has little or nothing at all to do with family feeling or has one heard that the children of wealthy parents are tied more to their parents than those of poor parents, or do rich parents love their children more than less well-to-do? What is indeed more important for the children, that the parents allow as good an education as possible to take root in them and allow them to learn something sound, educate them into industrious and healthy and brave men or that they leave them as big a bag of money as possible? In particular a justified effort to secure the future of their children even financially will no doubt have to be recognised. This effort, that is the habit of the parents of saving for their children, is in no way affected negatively by the breaking of interest slavery, on the contrary. The possibility of savings will become greater when our national economy is freed of the all encompassing pressure of interest slavery. We have indeed seen in the example of the man with 10,000 marks earnings and 5000 marks pension income that all medium and small wealth is in fact robbed of every advantage through the indirect route of the direct and indirect taxes of the house-interest, etc. I cannot repeat it too often: The loan interest of small and medium wealth is a swindle, a self-deception, a going round in circles, but big loan capital has diabolically enough propagated and announced throughout the world, through the press that is dedicated to it, the belief in the sanctity and inviolability of interest. It allows every man to apparently participate in the fine, numbing enjoyment of interest in order to euthanise the bad conscience that must unfailingly be connected with the indolent work-free enjoyment of interest - In order to acquire comrades in arms when it is a question of defending this highest good of Mammonism.

The official, the statesman will say: The state cannot break free from the debt that it has once entered into, and from its creditors.

What are debts? Is it perhaps more moral to incur debts about which the state must know from the start that it can fulfil these obligations only if it pays the interest to the creditors, to precisely the same amount, through taxes in either a direct or indirect way – where is the morality in that? Or is not perhaps much more honest to admit that: I can pay the interests only if I collect as much tax, but at that time, during the war, I definitely had to have money and that is why I conducted the swindle with the war-bonds; forgive me, dear people, it was indeed finally for you, and now I do not wish to hide anything any longer, I the state do not pay any taxes, and you, the tax-payer, do not need to pay any taxes for interests, that essentially simplifies our business. We save ourselves the enormous tax apparatus and likewise the extraordinary interest payment apparatus. Right, done? And you, Mr. Scheidemann,[31] do not any more set up on every advertisement column your name, as State Secretary of the old compromised government, under the fatuous statements relating to the security and inviolability of the war bonds. You compromised only yourself, only the large capital has the profit from the entire swindle.

The finance politicians and banking specialists will consider the breaking of the interest slavery of war bonds and debts as impossible because this would be synonymous with state bankruptcy.

I am sorry – we are indeed, or must become, bankrupt anyway according to their speeches. A public state bankruptcy would however be the most stupid thing that we could do; it would prematurely bring to the actual incapacity of the present power-holders also the historical confirmation of this incapacity.

Why then should one declare bankruptcy when I have thrust my 3 marks from my right trouser-pocket into my left, and therefore do not have to declare the bankruptcy of my right trouser-pocket!

But it was indeed not different with the war-bonds! The Reich removed from the pockets of the people the first actually existing billions, then the monies flowed back again; then came the new loan and again the money streamed back; then came the pump and sucked up the billions, and they ebbed again until, fortunately, after the game was played out nine times and the state had incurred a debt of 100 billion. For that the people had 100 billion of already printed paper in their hand. At first it was imagined that so and so had become much richer, then came

---

31 [Philipp Scheidemann (1865-1939) was a German Social Democratic politician who was the first to declare the formation of the Weimar Republic in November 1918. In February 1919, he became Chancellor but resigned in June due to his opposition to the Treaty of Versailles. He continued his political career as Mayor of Kassel (1920-1925) and moved to Denmark in 1933.]

the state and said: "It is frightful, I have debts to a 100 billion and am faced with bankruptcy". But why then? That is only a self-deception. I myself however can never become bankrupt if I move my money as often as possible from one pocket to the other. So, with regard to the state bankruptcy, with regard to our internal war-bond debts we can be quite reassured. That is why we really do not need to declare any state bankruptcy and spare ourselves the enormous work with the interests and the huge, though stupider, taxes. Let us finally free ourselves from worrying about the affairs of large loan capital! Except that only large loan capital has a benefit from this loan-interest-tax swindle for to it there remains a fine chunk of money and the working people pay this surplus in the form of indirect taxes; the smaller and medium capitalist however is turned around as a result.

The international economist says: The breaking of interest slavery is not possible to be introduced solely among us in Germany; that must be done internationally or we will lose all credit, capital flows away, and we must yet fulfil our interest obligations with regard to foreign countries.

I admit that I myself was not clear for a very long time on this question. It is the most difficult question because it brings us into a reciprocal relationship with the rest of the world – however the matter has two sides. First, the idea of the breaking of interest slavery is the battle-cry of all productive nations against the international financial slavery to interest and, secondly, it is the radical remedy for our internal financial misery. But there is really no reason not to make use of a remedy just because our nearest neighbour does not use it at the same time. It would however be wilful stupidity if we in Germany rotate deeper into the insane circle and pay taxes and interest when we have clearly recognised that this painful activity is exclusively for the benefit of the big capitalist. So let us go ahead with our liberating example, let us free ourselves from the financial slavery to interest, and we will soon see that the power of this victorious liberating idea will motivate the nations of the world to follow us.

I am indeed so convinced of it that our beginning – if this beginning is not suppressed by the German Mammonists – will pull the other nations along with irresistible necessity.

The Spartacist[32] says: The entire idea boils down just to a preservation

---

32   [The Spartakus Bund (Spartacus League) was founded by the Jews Karl

of capital, then things remain as before, the poor man has nothing and the rich remain.

Yes, my friend, it is in general very hard to discuss with you when you are, in the depths of your heart, a Communist, thus really wish that "everything should belong to everybody", when you know and consider as right even the actual thoughts of the big Bolshevik leaders in Russia, especially Lenin, thus consider the "universal accounting and control of the entire production and distribution" that has been designated as the next tasks of the Soviet Republic as humanly possible. But if you are absolutely clear of the fact that this task is realisable, if at all, only in the most frightening tyranny, and then you still remain in heart of hearts a convinced Communist or Spartacist, etc., then we do not wish to quarrel between ourselves, then we do not understand each other at all, we speak a foreign language and the future will decide on a strait-jacket state that may emerge finally from the Bolshevist chaos or the state hoped for by me with a national economy freed from interest slavery. But you, on account of your Communist soul – if you are honest, still have thoughts, longing for wife and child, for a human soul who stands closer to you than an eskimo or a Zulu kaffir,[33] if, at your factory work ordered by the Soviet leader, you think it would indeed be good to own a small house of your own, a small piece of garden of your own, if it does not, in the depths of your heart, give you real satisfaction that, like a dog on the street, you are entitled to use any bitch, I mean woman, running your way, if only you think of saving something of your pay for yourself that may then belong to you alone, then you are already no longer a Communist, then you have in your heart broken with your very loudly proclaimed catch-word "All things belong to all", then you do not indeed wish that everything belong to everybody, you wish that precisely that which you wish for yourself, wife, child, house, yard, savings, whether you already have it or just hope to obtain it, should then belong to you alone. And you see, my friend, if you doubt, even if only in the depths, that it would not be indifferent to you if just anybody came to you and, in the name of "all", simply took away from you that which you have saved, brought

---

Liebknecht (son of Wilhelm Liebknecht, founder of the SPD), Rosa Luxembourg and others as a revolutionary Marxist movement during the first World War. It later changed its name to Kommunistische Partei Deutschlands (KPD) and joined the Comintern in 1919. The same night that Schiedemann of the SPD declared a republic from the Reichstag (see above p.3), Liebknecht declared a Free Socialist Republic. However, the Spartacists were combated and defeated by President Ebert's centrist SPD.]

33   [A derogatory South African term for a negro.]

you another child and took yours with him, because all children belong to "all", then already, my friend, we shall not any longer be talking to each other at cross purposes, then I may perhaps request you to think whether the Communist message that all things should belong to all must not mean the end of all culture, that the lack of all concept of possession must with compelling logic push man down to the level of the animal.

If everything belongs to everybody, if in the best case a check and accounting of the entire official production and distribution in Lenin's sense were imposable, then there will result therefrom, in the best case, a state of ants. But then we can abandon language too, surrender our soul, our mind, dumb and instinctively we can accomplish our forced labour. That is the end of mankind.

But enough now, friend Spartacus. Let this fundamental consideration go right through your head and heart. A more precise answer to your question will be produced by discussion with the other parties.

And now, you comrades of both the socialist directions, centrists and independents!

I cannot imagine that a serious contradiction or objections would be made from your side against the breaking of interest slavery and yet I must discuss things with you fundamentally, with the entire socialist world of ideas, beginning with Marx up to the present leaders Ebert,[34] Scheidemann, Kautzky, etc.

The socialist Will: The uplifting of the working class is a definitely winning idea; so far we are together.

The ways entered upon to reach this great goal are almost completely false because they are built on false presuppositions.

The socialist idea of the state leads logically to Communism, thus to the downfall.

But because Social Democracy has another goal, an uplifting of the working class, generally of the entire working population, it now stands

---

34 [Friedrich Ebert (1871-1925) was a German Social Democratic politician who served as President of the Weimar Republic from February 1919 until his death.]

before a frightful internal cleavage because the logical consequences from Marxism lead directly to the opposite of what the practical goal of the workers' movement is.

Out of the internal conflict is produced the public uncertainty in the leadership of the government.

A strong line must be drawn against Spartacism and Bolshevist Communism on account of the great practical goal (uplifting of the working class) and their methods must be fought with all force. But Social Democracy organised in trade unions finds itself weak in the face of these radical groups because it has adopted the Marxist way of thought as an educational principle and because all Marxist thought processes lead to Communism.

Now the proof: Point 2 says that the ways entered upon by Social Democracy are almost completely false.

The almost universally adopted sedition has led to a deep division of the population within their own nation, the ever repeated invective against employers of all sorts, indeed of every bourgeois profession in general, as an exploiter and blood-sucker of the supposedly solely toiling worker has led to an unjustified embitterment and also to the idolisation of the worker which today consequently finds its expression in the demand of the "dictatorship of the proletariat" (Communist Manifesto). The most important demand of the Erfurt Programme[35] - the transfer of the means of production from private possession into the possession and operation of the community - has been concentrated today in the cry for "socialisation".

That the total socialisation of our economic downfall signifies total bankruptcy is fully clear to every honest politician. But one dares not admit this openly and freely to the people.

Not socialisation but de-socialisation ought to be the solution now. Thus one seeks to compensate for the obvious failures of every socialisation through fantastic tax projects and in this way to expropriate the expropriators a second time. But all that means nothing but surrendering the entire national economy to the inexorable downfall. Instead of an uplifting (there can in general be no talk at all of a doubling of production such as the entire socialist literature

---

35   [See above p.25]

promised for the period after the revolution), the exact opposite has occurred. But the worst would be if the present socialist government were to think of the acceptance of greater foreign loans. Therewith not only our economic downfall would be sealed, we would also be totally forced into interest slavery to the Entente, from which there would be no more return.

The fundamental mistake, the fundamental error on which this entire erroneous chain of conclusions, demands and promises to the people is built is the entirely false attitude towards industry - and loan capital. The Communist Manifesto, the Erfurt Programme, Marx, Engels, Lassalle,[36] Kautzky, have not recognised the deep difference between industry capital and loan capital.

On this point the entire Social Democracy must relearn, this fundamental error must be clearly recognised and admitted unreservedly, without half-measures. But then one must also uncompromisingly draw the only possible conclusion. But this means a radical rejection of the senseless – because entirely false – raging against industry, employers; workers and employers belong together, they have the same goal, work, production, for, without production, without work no life, no culture, no forwards and no upwards. The oppositions that are obvious because they are unavoidable among men – as long as they are men - are much less important than the great common interest of employer and employee. These oppositions can and could be solved by way of wage agreement and entrepreneurial organisation to the satisfaction of both sides.

However we do not wish to pursue these incidental questions within the scope of our observation of the rather wide political guidelines and declare once again that the interest of the entire workforce is quite exactly aligned with our national industry, with our national political economy.

One who teaches otherwise and places the oppositions between employers and workers in the foreground as being more important sins, in an irresponsible way, precisely against the workers for he lays therewith the axe to the roots of the tree that nourishes and supports the workers.

---

36 [Ferdinand Lassalle (1825-1864) was a German Jewish socialist who participated in the German Revolutions of 1848 and founded the Allgemeiner Deutscher Arbeiterverein (German Workers' Association) in 1863 to secure universal manhood suffrage.]

But Social Democracy has done that and therewith it has drawn upon itself eternal guilt with regard to the German workers, therewith it has brought a nameless misery upon our people, because it cannot fulfil all its promises, because it cannot bring us the peace of rapprochement, because it cannot create any work for us, because it must nevertheless set up an armed might once again, because it cannot manage without the bureaucracy, because it must demand obligatory work, because no man can live on universal equal and direct voting rights for men and women above the age of 20, because, without the state guaranteed security of person and property, chaotic conditions must emerge, because, without classification and ranking of the individual within society, no state life is possible.

Thus a deep desperate wave of disappointment passes over the entire nation, even if the individual has for a long time not been clear about it, so ministers, deputies and state commissioners continue to lie to themselves happily that one must protect the "accomplishments of the revolution" from the "reaction", both concepts about which no honest statesman can say clearly to the people what he means thereby.

The negative activities of the revolution, the deposition of a series of dynasties that had survived, deposition of officers, abolition of the aristocracy, dissolution of the army, in short, the great "demolition" is indeed no accomplishment. And reaction?! The decayed divine right of kings that was swept away did not have sufficient moral support anywhere in the entire nation to have been able to rise to any powerful action, the citizenry are, as far as it is a matter of the real bourgeoisie, much too cowardly, much too morally mired, to bestir themselves against class-conscious workers, so the leading class of the workers do not need to have any apprehension about a dynastic or bourgeois reaction.

But the deep disappointment of the people about the so-called accomplishments of the revolution, that is, about the lack of any improvement of the condition of the people, that is the great danger; this disappointment leads to the continued swarming of great masses of the people to the left, where that which existed of promises up to now is far surpassed, or undercut.

Finally one can do nothing more than promise "everything to everybody". And that is sheer madness; but every idea, every phenomenon, every activity extends and foments into its opposite. In this way also does it happen with the Communist idea that everything should belong to everybody, for this then finally ends and results in the fact that everybody has – nothing. Hunger, desperation, misery, illness and distress have set in in Russia, men have lost the last part of their courage to live and joy in living.

I repeat: The enormous fundamental mistake in the world of socialist ideas is in the final analysis is to be traced back to the disregard of the deep essential difference between industrial capital and loan capital. The interest-consuming loan capital is the scourge of mankind, the eternal effortless and endless growth of big loan capital - not the creative, goods-producing industrial entrepreneurial capital - leads to the exploitation of the nations.

Here I cannot pass by an investigation of the question why this essential difference has not been recognised; whether it has really not been recognised, or whether it has perhaps been veiled over entirely in favour of the big loan capital, whether the leaders and criers of the struggle against capitalism, whether the authors of the Communist Manifesto, of the Erfurt Programme, the present leaders, have always proceeded with the necessary conscientiousness.

It is the hardest and direst thing when one strictly raises a doubt about the absolute honesty and conviction of another, this is so much harder for one the more carefully one investigates by oneself the reasons and interconnections with regard to the phenomena of life. Therefore I shall give no answer to this question myself but only point to great dark interrelations by referring to a statement of Disraeli, the great English Prime Minister Lord Beaconsfield.

He writes in his novel *Endymion*:[37]

> No one will treat with indifference the principle of race. It is the key of history, and why history is often confused is that it has been written by men who were ignorant of this principle and all the knowledge it involves.

The Middle Class

The member of the middle class to whom peace is counted as a citizen's duty, is certainly frightened - as always by any new idea - by any new revolutionary demand, it means for him unrest, for he must thereby perhaps think of something. Every change is hateful to him, he wishes

---

37   [See Benjamin Disraeli, *Endymion*, Ch.IV.]

to have peace,[38] and woe to the one who wants his money-purse. Now one wishes to take his interests, his house interest, his security interests, his mortgage interests, that which is his peace, pleasure and happiness.

So we must then still find out what the members of the classes owning loan capital will have to say. But they form, apart from the real bourgeois – the bourgeois is a human type with whom nothing more can be expected at all, the bourgeois is a branch of the tree of mankind that should be cut off, the sooner the better, these are the sated, smug philistines with their wretched world-view, men who, incapable of any enthusiasm, pass their days in eternal monotony with coffee, morning newspaper, morning pint, afternoon newspaper, lunch, afternoon nap, cutting vouchers, evening pint, regulars' table at the pub, at best the cinema, with incomprehension of all that moves the world, what youth longs for, what is essential for the people, the state, the society, mindless of war and victory, mired down and duped, arrogant and servile at the same time – such a broad class that they cannot be ignored.

So: Through the breaking of interest slavery the savings habit is destroyed, a person ends up in a poorhouse.

That the breaking of interest slavery quite generally has an influence on the savings habit must definitely be denied. The savings habit has as little to do with valid economic views as waste, for example, does. The savings habit and addiction to waste are human characteristics that are either already present or missing, no matter whether an age preaches the idea of interest or prohibits interest.

In the times of transition either a rising or lowering of the savings habit can arise. But in the given case I tend much more to the view that a reasonable economically practical man would say to himself the following: I can in future no longer reckon that I can live only on my interests. But I wish to live in later age and also leave something to my children, so I must save more now." This effect the breaking of the interest slavery must, in my opinion, exert on the majority of men, for, otherwise they would indeed be dependent on public support in old age. I must even here expressly emphasise once again that, with the present burdening of property through direct taxes

---

38   [Feder spells peace (Ruhe) here as Ruah, the Hebrew word for the spirit of God.]

and of every living standard through indirect taxes, nothing will remain of the fine interests, except if – and that is the unjust thing that has to be combated – the entire income comes solely from eternal capital pension; so a lowering of the savings habit is perhaps not to be feared.

Is the (detestable) large capital then really so unfruitful, has it not also created the means towards great advancements which bear fruits for mankind that are greater than the amount constituted by the interest of loan capital?

No! The posing of the question only proves that the Mammonistic terminology has afflicted our clear sight.

Large capital has not created the means to great advancements but large capital has grown from work! Every capital is stored up work. Large capital is in itself unproductive because money in itself is a completely unfruitful thing. Values are created from spirit, work and existing or already processed raw materials and natural resources, and goods are produced through work and work alone.

For, if one poured in no matter how much money into the most fertile field, into the richest coal mine, the field does not bear for that reason any corn, the mine does not spew out any coal by itself! That we wish to state finally.

If money was invented that is very significant and intelligent; for in every complicated economy one requires this (universally recognised) "acknowledgement of performed work". But that in this "wealth" there should be an innate power to keep on growing from itself immeasurably – that money does when it can bear interest - that is what our innermost selves reject, that is what raises money far above all other earthly phenomena, that is what makes money an idol. And all that is only the greatest self-deception of mankind! By itself money can do nothing, absolutely nothing. A table, cupboard, clothing, house, tool, in short everything around us indeed has some value; one can finally burn the oldest table and warm oneself at it, but with a twenty mark coin I can do nothing at all, I cannot even develop a piece of cheese from it. Only after men have sensibly agreed, with regard to the facilitating of the exchange of consumer goods, to write out acknowledgements of performed work, only then does the slip of paper obtain a significance and purpose and it is very reasonable that a peasant receives from the coal mine not a piece of coal for his corn but money, an acknowledgement of work performed in another way, for example, with pitchforks, harness, plough and scythe. But therewith the power of money is over.

So, money has not effected the great advances of mankind but men themselves have done that, their dauntless spirit, their proud daring, their clever mind, the power of their hands, their common, that is, socially industrious work. So proudly and clearly must we consider things. It was men themselves, and not the wretched slip of paper that men invented for the simplification of economics.

Further Programme

But the breaking of interest slavery is not the final goal of the new statecraft, though it is the most decisive act that can unite all nations into a genuine federation of nations against the tyranny of Mammonism encompassing all nations. But it is not the final one. On the other hand, the breaking of interest slavery must precede all further steps because, as we have seen, it seizes the international evil at its roots, indeed at its tap-root.

Only when the fundamental demand for the breaking of interest slavery is fulfilled will the way be free to the social state. This must be recognised clearly and enforced in spite of all the mammonistic powers. A socialist state on a Mammonistic basis – the cry for socialisation is further nothing but the attempt to bring about the transformation of all industries into trusts and develop giant corporations everywhere on which also naturally, in the future, in spite of all expenditures of wealth, large loan capital will once again have the decisive influence – is a nonsense and leads with natural necessity to a compromise between the already strongly Mammonistically contaminated Social Democracy and large capital.

We on the other hand demand a radical rejection of the Mammonistic state and a construction of the state in the true spirit of socialism in which the ruling basic idea is the nourishing duty in which an old Communistic fundamental demand may find its reasonable and sensible satisfaction in the form that every member of the nation is awarded his claim to his native soil through the state distribution of the most important food products.

We demand further, as a framework for the new state, popular representation through the chamber of national commissioners who are to be voted on the widest possible basis, and along with that a corporative chamber of labour, the central council, in which the working people have a say according to their professional ranking and economic structure. Finally we demand the highest responsibility for the leaders of the state. Another work that will appear soon from the same publishers will deal with this new state structure on a socialistic-aristocratic foundation.[39] But the precondition for all this building up remains the breaking of the interest slavery.

My unshakeable belief, nay more, my knowledge allows me to clearly recognise that the breaking of interest slavery is not only enforceable but will and must also be adopted everywhere with indescribable jubilation, for let it be clearly observed: In contrast to all other well-intentioned ideas and movements and efforts that aim at an improvement of the human race, my plan does not seek to improve human nature but it is directed against a poison, against a phenomenon that has been invented artificially, nay diabolically, against the deepest feeling of man to make mankind sick, to entangle it deep in materialism in order to rob it of the best possession that it has, its soul. Along with it goes hand in hand the frightful, ruthless tyranny of the financial powers for whom men are only interest slaves, who are there only to work for annuities, for interest.

Deeply shocked we recognise the frightful clarity and truth of the old biblical prophecies according to which the Jewish god Jehovah promises to his chosen people: "I will give you all the treasures of the world as your own, all the nations should lie at your feet, and you shall rule over them".

This world question has now unfurled itself before you all. World questions are not solved in a trice but the idea is clear as day. And the act must be carefully prepared, we must be clear about the fact that we stand before the most powerful enemy, the world-encompassing financial powers. All power on the opponents' side, on our side only right, the eternal right of productive work.

Give me your hands, workers of all lands, unite!

---

39   [Feder's next work, *Der deutsche Staat auf nationaler und sozialer Grundlage* was published in 1923.]

Bibliography

Gottfried Feder: Major Works

Das Manifest zur Brechung der Zinsknechtschaft des Geldes, Munich, 1919.

(with A. Buckeley), *Der kommende Steuerstreik; Seine Gefahr, seine Unvermeidlichkeit, seine Wirkung*, Diessen, 1921.

Der deutsche Staat auf nationaler und sozialer Grundlage; Neue Wege in Staat, Finanz und Wirtschaft, Munich, 1923.

Das Programm Der NSDAP und seine weltanschaulichen Grundlagen, Munich, 1927.

The Programme Of The NSDAP And Its General Conceptions, tr. E.T.S. Dugdale, Munich, 1932.

Die Juden, Munich, 1933.

Kampf gegen die Hochfinanz, Munich, 1933.

(with F. Rechenberg) *Die Neue Stadt. Versuch der Begründung einer neuen Stadtplanungskunst aus der sozialen Struktur der Bevölkerung*, Berlin, 1939.

Secondary Literature

Avraham Barkai, *Wirtschaftliche Grundanschauungen und Ziele der NSDAP (mit einem unveröffentlichen Dokument aus dem Jahr 1931)*, *Jahrbuch des Instituts für deutsche Geschichte*, VII (1978).

Avraham Barkai, *Nazi Economics: Ideology, Theory And Policy*, Oxford, 1990.

W.A. Boelcke, *Die deutsche Wirtschaft 1930-1945*, Düsseldorf, 1983.

Andre Bories, *Gottfried Feder und sein Einfluss auf das Wirtschaftsprogramm der NSDAP*, (e-book), Munich, Grin Verlag, 2005.

R. Erbe, *Die nationalsozialistische Wirtschaftspolitik 1933-9 im Lichte der modernen Theorie*, Zurich, 1958.

Bibliography

C. Guillebaud, *The Economic Recovery Of Germany 1933-1938*, London, 1939.

G. Hallgarten, "Adolf Hitler and German heavy industry 1931-1933", *Journal of Economic History*, 12 (1952).

A. Herrmann, Gottfried Feder. *Der Mann und sein Werk*, Leipzig, 1933.

H. James, *The German Slump: Politics And Economics 1924-1936*, Oxford, 1986.

B.H. Klein, *Germany's Economic Preparations For War*, Harvard University Press, 1968.

Christian Körber, Gottfried Feder; *Der Programmatiker der Bewegung* (e-book), Munich, Grin Verlag, 2005.

Werner Krause, *Wirtschaftstheorie unter dem Hakenkreuz; Die bürgerliche Ökonomie in Deutschland unter der faschistischen Herrschaft*, Berlin, 1967.

Christina Kruse, *Die Volkswirtschaftslehre im Nationalsozialismus*, Freiburg, 1988.

A.S. Milward, *The German Economy At War*, London, 1965

Richard Overy, *The Nazi Economic Recovery 1932-1938*, 1st ed. Macmillan, 1982, 2nd. ed. Cambridge University Press, 1996.

A. Tyrell, "Gottfried Feder and the NSDAP", in: P. D. Stachura, *The Shaping of the Nazi State*, London, 1978.

A. Tyrell, "Gottfried Feder - Der gescheiterte Programmatiker", in: Smelser/Zitelmann, *Die braune Elite*, Darmstadt, 1989.

Helmut Woll, *Die Wirtschaftslehre des deutschen Faschismus*, München, 1994.

Lightning Source UK Ltd.
Milton Keynes UK
UKOW06f2324160616

276487UK00016B/335/P